Hello Visual Basic

An Introduction to Programming
with
Microsoft® Visual Basic™ 3.0

Janet E. Joy

Publications

Hello World Publications
P.O. Box 2830
Silver Spring MD 20915   USA

PUBLISHED BY
Hello World Publications
P.O. Box 2830
Silver Spring, MD 20915

Phone: (301) 942-4277
Fax Phone: (301) 933-6488

ISBN 0-9648160-0-8

Manufactured in the United States of America

Trademark Acknowledgments
All terms mentioned in this book that are known to be trademarks or service marks are listed below. In addition, terms suspected of being trademarks or service marks have been appropriately capitalized. Hello World Publications cannot attest to the accuracy of this information. Use of a term in this book should not be regarded as affecting the validity of any trademark or service mark.

dBase is a registered trademark of Borland International, Inc.
Hewlett-Packard is a registered trademark of Hewlett-Packard Company.
FoxPro, Microsoft, Microsoft Access, Microsoft Excel, and MS-DOS are registered trademarks.
Visual Basic and Windows are trademarks of Microsoft Corporation.
All other trademarks and service marks are the property of their respective owners.

Limits of Liability and Disclaimer of Warranty
The author and publisher of this book have used their best efforts in preparing this book and the programs contained in it. The author and publisher make no warranty of any kind, expressed or implied, with regard to the programs or the documentation contained in this book. The author and publisher shall not be liable in any event for incidental or consequential damages in connection with, or arising out of, the performance, or use of these programs.

In Memory of My Father

John L. Joy

Contents

Notation Used in this Book

Tab : A box around a word indicates a key on the keyboard to press. Press the key labeled TAB, do *not* type T-a-b. Other keys used include **Ctrl**, **Alt**, and **↵Enter**

Ctrl+C : A key followed by a plus sign and a letter indicates that you should hold down the key with the box around it, type the letter, then release both keys. *(Similar to holding down* **Shift** *to type an uppercase letter.)*

```
form1.caption="Hello"
```

Text inside a shaded box indicates code to be entered exactly as shown.

<integer value> : Text written in italics inside these brackets indicate a general category. This would be replaced by a value such as 5 or 238.

<variable> = *<expression>* could be written as X=5, where X is a variable and 5 is an expression.

⇨ : When a line of code does not fit on a printed page, the arrow ⇨ indicates that you should not press **↵Enter** but continue typing as one line of code. The next line will begin with the ⇨ symbol:

```
Sub Form_MouseMove (Button As Integer, Shift As Integer, ⇨
    ⇨ X As Single, Y As Single)

End Sub
```

Select: The first item in a list is visible from the main menu, additional items in the list will appear in sub-menus. Selection can be made by clicking on the item, or by holding down and typing the underlined letter. Some selections are made from a dialog window, such as a file name or color.

Select <u>F</u>ile, Save File <u>A</u>s, name the file B:\HELLO.FRM

Select **File** from the main menu by clicking on it, or typing **Alt**+**F**;
From the sub-menu select **Save As** by clicking on it, or typing **Alt**+**A**;
From the File dialog window, select the **B:** drive, then name the file HELLO.FRM
(Click OK to leave the file dialog window.)

Suggestions

To get the most out of this book:
- Read the exercise through once;
- Go through the exercise at the computer and write the program;
- Close the book and write the program on your own;
- Make modifications to the program;
- Create an entirely different program using the same techniques.

About The Author

The author has taught Computer Science for the past 20 years at: College Of Staten Island, La Guardia Community College, Trenton State College, and Middlesex County College. She is currently an associate professor at Northern Virginia Community College.

Chapter 0

Introduction

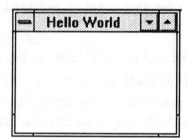

Hello World

Learn About the Visual Basic Programming Environment

Write the First Program: "Hello World"

Change the Color & Caption at Run Time

Use HELP

What Is Visual Basic?

Visual Basic is an *object oriented* programming language. It is used to write Windows programs that are GUI and event driven. It's WHAT???

GUI: *Graphical User Interface* (pronounced gooey): the user can make choices with the mouse rather than having to type everything. He selects icons Hello World , option buttons ⊙ command buttons ⎡ E**x**it ⎤, and other *graphic* images, or pictures.

Object: An object combines both data (properties) and events (procedures). You will *build* your program from objects such as forms, command buttons, scroll bars, text boxes and timers. Each object (or *control*) has properties such as a name, width, color and font. You write code for events that may happen to the control. Some of the events that can happen include click on it, double click it, or move the mouse over it, the user types in a text box, or a timer goes off. Different kinds of objects have different properties and events associated with them. For example, scroll bars have maximum and minimum properties; while a timer has an interval property. Text boxes have properties such as font, font color and font size. Most properties can be changed at both design time and at run time.

Event Driven: When you run an event driven program, it continuously checks to see if an event has occurred. When an event occurs, any code for that event is executed, then the cycle of checking for another event continues.

Windows: When you start Windows, (type **WIN** and press ⎡◄Enter⎤ at the **C:\>** prompt), you should see the Win logo ▦. After a few seconds you will see the start-up window. Look for the word **Help**: the underlined **H** means that you can execute that command by typing the keys ⎡Alt⎤+**H**. *(Hold down* ⎡Alt⎤ *and press* **H**, *then release both keys.)* You can also execute the command by double-clicking on it. Help includes a tutorial on using Windows: if you have never used Windows you should find this tutorial helpful.

Windows Terms You Should Know

Click: Press down on the left mouse button and release it immediately.

Double-click: Click the left mouse button twice very quickly. If you don't do it fast enough it is just clicked twice - *not* double-clicked.

Mouse Pointer: When the mouse is moved, the mouse pointer ⬚ indicates the position on the screen. When you are in a text window, the mouse pointer becomes an *insertion* pointer: I, this indicates a point between two letters: clicking the mouse will allow you to insert text at that point. The mouse pointer becomes a double arrow at the borders of a window (*see below*).

Drag: As in "Drag the icon to the bottom of the screen": put the mouse pointer on top of the icon and press down on the left mouse button (don't release it). Now move the mouse to the specified location by dragging the mouse (and the icon with it) to the new location. Drop the icon by releasing the mouse button. A window can be dragged by its title bar.

Parts of the Window

All illustrations in this book are for Windows 3.1. Visual Basic works the same in Windows 95. The major difference in Windows 95 is the location of the maximize, minimize and control menu.

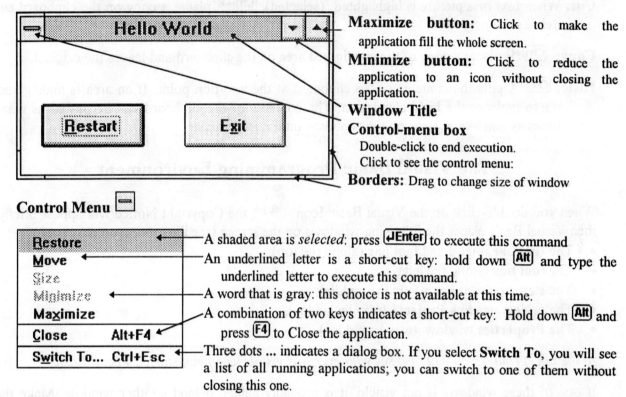

Maximize button: Click to make the application fill the whole screen.

Minimize button: Click to reduce the application to an icon without closing the application.

Window Title

Control-menu box
   Double-click to end execution.
   Click to see the control menu:

Borders: Drag to change size of window

Control Menu

A shaded area is *selected*: press ⏎**Enter** to execute this command

An underlined letter is a short-cut key: hold down **Alt** and type the underlined letter to execute this command.

A word that is gray: this choice is not available at this time.

A combination of two keys indicates a short-cut key: Hold down **Alt** and press **F4** to Close the application.

Three dots ... indicates a dialog box. If you select **Switch To**, you will see a list of all running applications; you can switch to one of them without closing this one.

Highlighted Selections: In the "Hello World" application shown above, the **Restart** button has a darker border than the **Exit** button, the dark border indicates that Restart has been selected. Pressing ⏎**Enter** will execute the code for the Restart button. You can select the **Exit** button by clicking on it, or (*usually*) by pressing **Tab**. In the Control menu , the word **Restore** is highlighted, pressing ⏎**Enter** will execute Restore (Restore the window to its original size).

Changing the Size of a Window by Dragging: When the mouse is on a border of a window it changes to a double arrow:

⇔ on the vertical edges - press down on the left mouse button and drag to make the window wider or narrower.

⇕ on the horizontal edges - press down on the left mouse button and drag to make the window shorter or taller.

⤢ on the corners - press down on the left mouse button and drag the mouse at an angle to change both dimensions.

The Clipboard

The Clipboard is used to copy text and pictures from one location to another.

Cut: When text or a picture is highlighted (selected), `Ctrl`+**X** places a copy on the clipboard and **deletes** the original.

Copy: `Ctrl`+**C** places a copy of the highlighted area on the clipboard and leaves the original.

Paste: `Ctrl`+**V** puts the contents of the clipboard at the insertion point. If an area is highlighted, **paste** replaces the highlighted area. The contents of the clipboard can be pasted as many times as you like: it stays on the clipboard until it is replaced.

The Visual Basic Programming Environment

When you double-click on the Visual Basic Icon, the Copyright Notice will appear briefly, then Visual Basic places the following windows on the screen (see illustration on next page):
- The **title bar, menu** and **tool bar** (along the top):
- The **tool box** (along the left);
- The start-up form: **Form1** (in the middle);
- The project window **Project1** (may be hidden);
- The **Properties** window. (may be hidden)

In the background, you will also see whatever was visible when you started Visual Basic.

If one of these windows is not visible, it is probably hidden behind another window. Make the following selection from the menu to view a window that is not visible:

Toolbar: from menu select `View`, `Toolbar`.
Toolbox: select `Window`, `Toolbox`.
Project: select `Window`, `Project`
Properties: select `Window`, `Properties`
Form: select `View Form` from Project Window.

(There are a few other windows: they will be discussed later in this book.)

The ToolBar

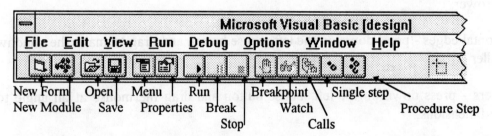

Do not worry if some of the names are confusing- by the time you finish this book, all of the tools on the tool bar *will be familiar to you!*

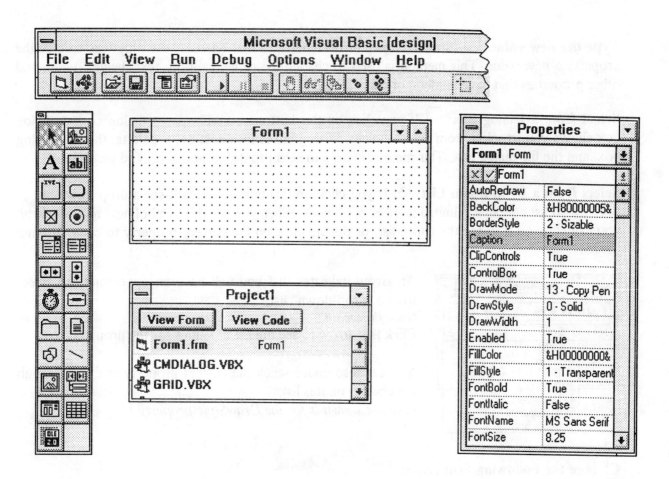

The First Program: "Hello World"

Changing the Properties Of The Form: When Form1 is visible, the property icon 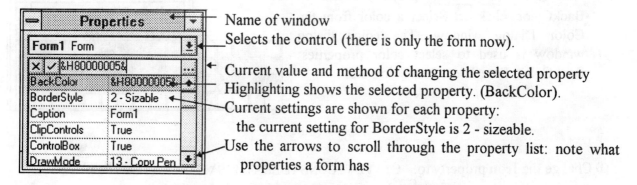 on the top tool bar is enabled. (The icons on enabled buttons are black; disabled buttons have light gray icons.) Click on the property icon. The property window will appear:

— Name of window
—Selects the control (there is only the form now).

◄— Current value and method of changing the selected property
—Highlighting shows the selected property. (BackColor).
—Current settings are shown for each property:
   the current setting for BorderStyle is 2 - sizeable.
—Use the arrows to scroll through the property list: note what
   properties a form has

Changing the Value of a Property

You can change properties by clicking on the property and then giving it a new value. When you select a property the current value and method of changing the value are shown. There are three methods to change the value of a property:

Type the new value: ⬒ (disabled down arrow) indicates that typing is the only way to give the property a new value. This method is used to change the name, caption, text, height, width and other properties that have numeric or text values.

Select from a Dialog Box: ⬚ If you click on this button you will open a dialog box. A dialog box allows you to select from many choices. Dialog boxes include a color palette, the font dialog box, and the file dialog box. This method is used to select fonts, colors, icons and pictures.

Select from a Drop Down List: ⬓ If you click on this button you will see a drop-down list. A drop down list contains a limited number of choices. When you see this symbol next to a property, you can click on it to see the entire list, or double-click on the current property to cycle through the list.

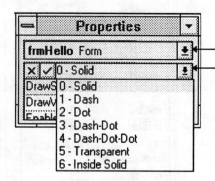

An arrow indicates that you will have an opportunity to select from a "drop-down" list.
Select the control
Click this arrow to see the list of values for the property.

You can also double-click the current property to cycle through the choices on this list.
(The list shown is for the DrawStyle property.)

Change the Following Properties:

① Change the **Name** property to `frmHello`: Scroll to Name, click, type **frmHello**

② Change the **Caption** property to `Hello World`: Click on Caption, type **Hello World** (The caption changes on the form as you type.)

③ Change the **BackColor** property: Click on BackColor, click ⬚ Select a color from the Color Dialog window. The color dialog window is used to select color properties: BackColor, ForeColor, FontColor, etc.

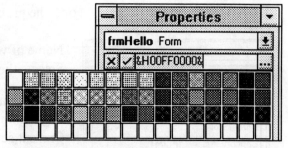

Hello World

④ Change the **Icon** property to: `C:\VB\ICONS\ELEMENTS\EARTH.ICO`
Click on Icon, click ⬚ to open a file Dialog window. Change to the `C:\VB\ICONS\ELEMENTS` directory to select the "Earth" icon. *(See Appendix D, page 179 if you do not know how to select a file from the file dialog window. All icons that you are asked to select come with Visual Basic.)* You will not see the icon at this time: you will see it when you minimize at run time.

This program does not draw anything, so the following change will not make any difference, but it gives you a chance to try the third method:

⑤ Change the **DrawStyle** property:

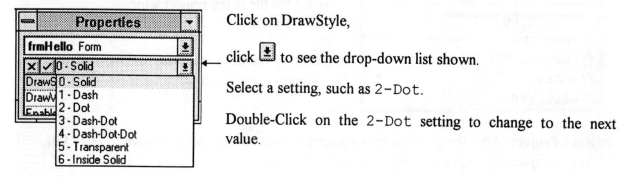

Click on DrawStyle,

click ⬇ to see the drop-down list shown.

Select a setting, such as 2-Dot.

Double-Click on the 2-Dot setting to change to the next value.

RUN the Program

In the middle of the top tool bar, there is a *RUN* button: ▶. Click the *RUN* button to start the program. The run button is now disabled (light gray) and the *STOP* button: ■ is enabled (black). The program doesn't have any code yet, but the window can be dragged, the size changed, and it can be minimized and maximized. When the program is minimized, the icon that was selected for the form replaces it. Clicking the icon will restore it to its original size.

STOP

There are three ways to stop execution, *try stopping the program each way:*

- Press 〔Alt〕+〔F4〕 (Hold down 〔Alt〕 and press the function key 〔F4〕);
- Click the control-menu box in the top left corner of a running application ⊟, select C̲lose;
- Click the STOP button ■ on the Visual Basic tool bar.

Save The Program

You should save each of your programs, even if the instructions don't specifically say to save.

⑥ Save **the Form**: If the project window is not visible select W̲indow, P̲roject
The project window has several files listed.

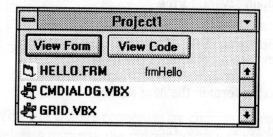

Select **frmHello** in the project window.

Select F̲ile, from the menu bar, then select
Save File A̲s...from the sub-menu.
Name the file B:\HELLO.FRM

The new name of the form will appear as shown

The name of the file on disk, HELLO.FRM is shown on the left. The name of the form frmHello, is on the right.

⑦ **Remove Files:** The project window has several files listed. The only file that the "Hello World" program uses is frmHello. All of the other files should be removed.

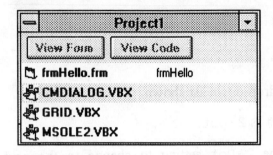

For each file that your project does not use:
Select the file in the project window:
(CMDIALOG.VBX is selected in the illustration.)

Select **F**ile, from the menu bar, then select **R**emove File from the sub-menu.

⑧ **Save Project:** After the all of the files except frmHello have been removed, select **File**, Sav**e** Project As... name the project B:HELLO.MAK.

The name of the form will now appear as the project title.

Create an Execute File

Select **F**ile, Ma**k**e Exe File..., name the file B:\HELLO.EXE (Visual Basic has probably already named it for you.)

If you selected an icon for the form, you will see it now. If the icon shown is the default icon for a form, ⌐, you can select Cancel to go back to the project and select an icon. When you minimize this project, this is the icon that will appear.

Note: If you intend to give your program to someone who does not have Visual Basic on their computer, include a copy of **C:\WINDOWS\SYSTEM\VBRUN300.DLL** on the disk.

Print The Program

To print your program, select **F**ile, from the menu bar, then select **P**rint

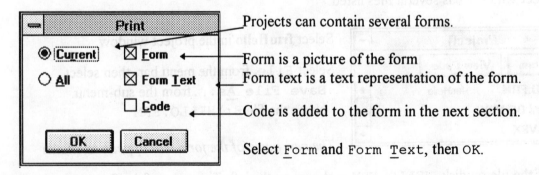

Projects can contain several forms.

Form is a picture of the form

Form text is a text representation of the form.

Code is added to the form in the next section.

Select **F**orm and Form **T**ext, then OK.

Saving an Unfinished Project

If you are working on a project and do not have time to finish, you can select `File`, then `Save File` or `Save File As` from the sub-menu. It you have added a new feature to the program and have not tested it yet, you may want to use `Save As` and give it a different name. If the new feature does not work, you can always go back to the first version.

Opening an Existing Project

When you select `File` from the menu bar, a list of the four most recent projects are shown at the bottom of the window. Click on the name of the project to open all of the files in the project.

You can also use buttons on the tool bar to open 🖿 and save 🖬 a project.

Require Variable Declaration

The first time you run Visual Basic, select **Options**, then **Environment**. The Environment Options window shown below will appear. Changes made to these settings will apply to all Visual Basic Programs until you change them again. Change **Require** Variable Declaration to **YES**, as shown in the illustration. This means that a variable can not be used if it has not been declared. (A safety measure!) Don't change other settings until you have used Visual Basic and know what your preferences are.

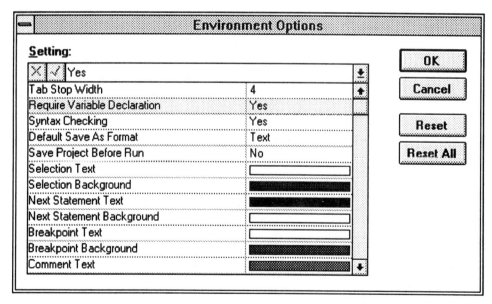

Adding Code To a Program

Start a New Project: Select `File`, `New Project` Change the Name property 🖹 of the form to frmOne. **Important:** Change the Name of the Form and any other controls (objects) before you add code!

Code View Window

Double click on the form to activate the CODE window, shown below.

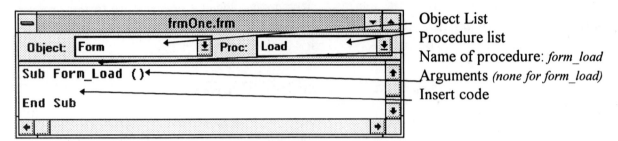

Object List
Procedure list
Name of procedure: *form_load*
Arguments *(none for form_load)*
Insert code

The Object List

The object that was double-clicked will appear in the object list window as the selected object. You doubled-clicked the form (it is the only object in the project at this point), therefore **Form** appears in the `Object:` window.

The name of a procedure is: *<name of the object>_<name of the event>*. The name of the procedure above is `Form_Load` (the *load* event for the *form* object).

Pull down the object list by pressing its down arrow ⊡. There are only two objects on the list, **Form** and **(general)**. As objects are added to the project this list will grow.

The Procedure List

Pull down the `Proc:` list by pressing its down arrow ⊡; you will see a list of every event (procedure) that can happen to a form. Scroll through them, you will see Click, DblClick, MouseMove, KeyPress and others. *(Names of objects, events and variables can not have a space, that is why names like MouseMove have no space, but use a capital letter to make it easier to understand the meaning.)*

Adding Code: To add code to an event, first select the object from the Object list, then select the procedure. Select Object: **Form**, Procedure: **Click.** The window shown below will appear. The name of this procedure is `Form_Click`. (The *click* event for the *form* object.)

From now on, when code is shown, you will be expected to find the procedure by its name.

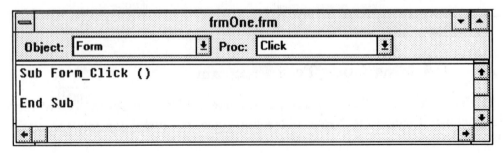

Add the line shown below. This procedure is executed when the mouse is clicked anywhere on the form, it will change the caption of the form to "You clicked the mouse". In Visual Basic it doesn't matter if you use upper case or lower case letter: **Caption** is the same as **caption** except inside quotes.

```
Sub Form_Click ()
   frmOne.Caption = "You clicked the mouse"
End Sub
```

Run the program. If the name of your form is not frmOne, you may get an error message when you try to run it. Correct the code, using the name of the form, then try running it again.

The Object List

Pull down the object list and select **(general)** at the top of the list. You should see the line **Option Explicit** shown below. This line is automatically inserted if you set the Environment option to Require Variable Declaration. If you do not see the line Option Explicit, type it as shown. Set the environment options as shown on the previous page. The next time you use Visual Basic, check to be sure that the line is being inserted automatically.

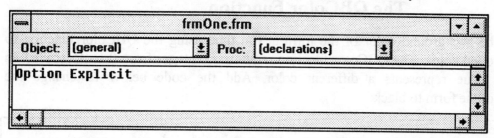

Add the code shown below, then run the program. **Caption** is the same as **frmOne.Caption** because frmOne is the *default*, if we don't specify which caption to change, it assumes we mean frmOne. Practice clicking and double-clicking.

```
Sub Form_DblClick ()
   caption = "Double Click"
End Sub
```

A Little Fun

The examples below allow you to explore the events of the form. Add the code shown in each example below, then run the program. Comments have been added to some of the code. Comments begin with a single quote ' . Comments have no effect on the execution, they are included to allow programmers to leave notes for themselves.

The Beep Command

If the program does not beep when the program starts, the sound on your computer may not be working, or has been disabled. Some schools have disabled sound on the computers because it can be distracting.

```
Sub Form_Load()    'the starting point for every program
   Beep
End Sub
```

The End Command

The **End** statement stops execution, this command allows the programmer to end the program instead of having the user stop execution.

```
Sub Form_DblClick ()
   End
End Sub
```

The QBColor Function

You can change the background color of the form at run time using the QBColor function to change the background color: The QBColor function requires an integer from 0 to 15 (called an *argument*). Each value represents a different color. Add the code below to change the background color of the form to black:

```
Sub Form_Click ()
   Caption = "You clicked the mouse"
   BackColor = QBColor(0) 'Change background color of form to black
End Sub
```

Try using other values for QBColor by changing the argument (the number in parenthesis). Use a different color for each event. Follow the steps below if you want to add the same line of code in several procedures:

- Type the line once;
- Drag the mouse over the line to highlight it;
- Type **Ctrl**+**C** *(this copies the line to the clipboard)*
- Select the procedure you want to add code to;
- Position the mouse pointer I where you want the code and click once;
- Type **Ctrl**+**V** (a copy of the code is now in the procedure)
- Change the QBColor value (this is the only part you have to type!)

Warning: The program will give you an error message if you try any values other than 0 to 15.

HELP!

Help Is Just a Click Away: Would you like to know what color the QBColor values stand for instead of guessing? Select <u>H</u>elp from the menu, select <u>S</u>earch for Help On... from the sub-menu, then type 'Q'. QBColor immediately appears in the selection box. Select QBColor and press ⏎**Enter** or click the **Go To** command. Help gives you a complete list of the 15 QBColors, plus examples and an explanation.

The Help Window:

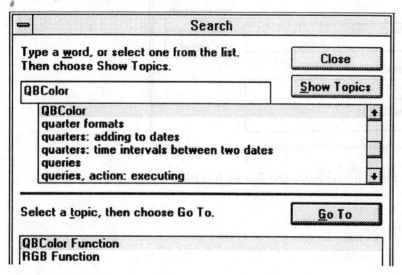

Note: The colors may be different on your monitor. This is a problem with the way monitors work, not with your program.

The RGB Function

More colors are available with the RGB function. The RGB function requires three arguments red, green and blue: **RGB(<*red*>, <*green*>, <*blue*>)** Values for red, green and blue can be from 0 to 255. Each pixel (point) is made up of these three colors. If all three values are 0 (none of the lights are on), the color will be black. If all three values are 255 (all the lights on full strength), the color will be white. *(You are mixing lights, not paints!)* The procedure below changes the background color to red and changes the caption when the mouse is double-clicked:

```
Sub Form_DblClick ()
  Caption = "Double Click"
  BackColor = RGB(255, 0, 0)
End Sub
```

Experiment

Try changing the RGB arguments to produce red when the mouse is clicked and green when the mouse is double clicked. Display a caption of "STOP" or "GO".

Write code for several procedures: Beep when you click, change to red when you double-click, and so on. You should spend some time becoming familiar with the procedures and properties of the form.

Viewing the Code

Procedures that have code attached are in bold face in the procedure list. A list of all coded procedures can be viewed and selected by selecting `Window`, `Procedures` from the menu bar, or by pressing [F2]:

Procedure List: **View Procedure Window:**

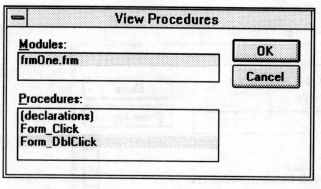

Remove all unnecessary files from the project. Save the file as `B:ONE.FRM`, save the project as `B:ONE.MAK`.

Chapter 1

A Closer Look At The Form

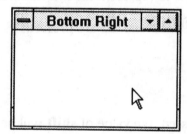

Learn About Arguments

Write IF ELSE Statements

Declare Variables

Use the "Debug" Window

Arguments

Some procedures receive arguments. The arguments that a procedure receives are shown in parenthesis after the procedure name. Arguments are variables, because the value can vary, or change. Variable names can not have a space in them, a capital letter is often used to make the name readable. Use of capital letters is optional: the variable **hours** is the same as **Hours**.

The **Form_MouseMove** procedure receives four arguments:

```
Sub Form_MouseMove (Button As Integer, shift As Integer, ⇨
    ⇨ x As Single, y As Single)

End Sub
```

Note: The ⇨ symbol indicates that the line continues: See Notation at front of book.

Button tells which mouse buttons (left, right, or middle) were pressed.

Shift tells which of the keys [Shift], [Ctrl] and [Alt] were pressed.

X and **Y** are the *position* of the mouse:
   X is the number of spaces over from the left, the column.
   Y is the number of spaces down, the row.
   (If you move the mouse to the top left corner, X and Y will both be zero.)

The arguments Shift and Button both use binary digits to represent the individual keys or buttons:

The argument **Shift** indicates which of the keys [Shift], [Ctrl] and [Alt] are pressed:
   [Shift] has a value of 1;
   [Ctrl] has a value of 2;
   [Alt] has a value of 4.

These values are added together: if only [Shift] is pressed, the value of **shift** will be 1. If both [Shift] and [Alt] are pressed, the value of shift will be 5. The table below shows the value of Shift for each combination of keys:

[Alt]	[Ctrl]	[Shift]	Value of Shift
no	no	no	0
no	no	yes	1
no	yes	no	2
no	yes	yes	3
yes	no	no	4
yes	no	yes	5
yes	yes	no	6
yes	yes	yes	7

The argument **Button** works the same way as Shift: The left mouse button has a value of 1; the right button has a value of 2; and the middle mouse button (*if you have one*) has a value of 4.

Middle	Right	Left	Value of Button
no	no	no	0
no	no	yes	1
no	yes	no	2
no	yes	yes	3
yes	no	no	4
yes	no	yes	5
yes	yes	no	6
yes	yes	yes	7

The **Form_KeyDown** procedure (shown below), receives two arguments: keycode (an integer) and shift. Shift is the same as above. **Keycode** indicates which key is being pressed (using the ANSI values).

```
Sub Form_KeyDown (keycode As Integer, shift As Integer)

End Sub
```

The procedures shown below change the caption to display the values of the arguments. When you want to display several values in a caption, use the **&** to *concatenate* the arguments *(add the strings together)*.

Example: The code in this exercise can be added to form1 without changing any properties. You do not need to save the project.

```
Sub Form_KeyDown (keycode As Integer, shift As Integer)
  Caption = "Key down: keycode=" & keycode & " Shift=" & shift
End Sub
```

If you press (Shift)+(Alt)+X at run time, the caption will be "Key down: keycode=88 Shift=5"

You could also write the procedure using two statements:

```
Sub Form_KeyDown (keycode As Integer, shift As Integer)
  Caption = "Key down: keycode=" & keycode
  Caption = Caption & " Shift=" & shift
End Sub
```

This time, if you press (Shift)+(Alt)+X at run time, the first statement:

Caption = "Key down: keycode=" & keycode assigns caption the value
"Key down: keycode= 88".

The second statement, **Caption = Caption & " Shift=" & shift** assigns a new value to caption by concatenating " Shift=5" to the current caption. The caption becomes
"Key down: keycode=88 Shift=5"

The code below shows the same method used in Form_MouseMove to display the arguments:

```
Sub Form_MouseMove (Button As Integer, shift As Integer, ◊
    ◊ x As Single, y As Single)
  Caption = "Mouse move: x=" & x
  Caption = Caption & " y=" & y
End Sub
```

The code below uses the value of shift to change the QBColor. This is OK because shift can't have a value bigger than 7. If you try to use one of the other variables in QBColor, your program will crash! *Save your program before you try it!*

```
Sub Form_KeyDown (keycode As Integer, shift As Integer)
  Caption = "Key down: keycode=" & keycode & " Shift=" & shift
  BackColor = QBColor(shift)
End Sub
```

Experiment: Add similar code to other procedures of the form that receive arguments.

Boolean Expressions

Sometimes a programmer would like one statement, or group of statements to execute only if certain conditions are true. There may be a different statement, or group of statements that are to be executed when the condition is false. An expression that can be evaluated to true or false is called a Boolean expression. (Named after a mathematician named Boole).

Examples of Boolean Expressions: *(X and Y are variables)*

X = 5	(True if X has a value equal to 5)
X > Y	(True if X is greater than Y; example X is 7, Y is 3)
X < Y	(True if X is less than Y; example X is 2, Y is 2.5)
X <> Y	(True if X is not equal to Y; example X is 5, Y is 6)
X >= Y	(X is greater than or equal to Y; example X is 4, Y is 3 or 4)
X <= Y	(X is less than or equal to Y; example X is 4, Y is 4 or 5)

Comparing Strings

Characters and strings can also be compared, because each character has an integer value. The letter "A" has a value that is *less than* the value of the letter "B". "Ann" is *less than* "Bill". When comparing strings, *less than* can be read as *"comes before alphabetically"*.
Caution: The integer 5 is less than the integer 10, but the string "5" is greater than the string "10", because strings are compared letter by letter. Captions are strings unless you use a function to convert the string to a number. *(See the function* **Val** *in Appendix E.)*

Examples:
```
Answer = "Y"
Answer <> "No"
SearchName < Name
```

The IF Statement

The IF..THEN statement is used to execute a statement only under certain conditions.

The format is: **If** _____ **Then** _____
                        Boolean   *Statement to execute*
                        expression   *if True*

Another way to show this format is:

```
If <Boolean exp.> Then <true statement >
```

Experiment: Run the program: move the mouse around to get it to beep. (You can leave the line to display the values of X and Y if you want.)

```
Sub Form_MouseMove (Button As Integer, Shift As Integer, ↩
   ↩ x As Single, y As Single)
 If x = y Then Beep
End Sub
```

ELSE: To execute a statement when the Boolean expression is False, use **ELSE**. The format is:

```
If <Boolean exp.> Then <true statement> Else <false statement>
```

Example:

```
Sub Form_MouseMove (Button As Integer, Shift As Integer, ↩
   ↩  x As Single, y As Single)
 If x < y Then BackColor = QBColor(0) Else BackColor = QBColor(5)
End Sub
```

Blocks: The **If...Then ... Else** statement shown above could also be written using *Blocks*. Notice that an If block requires **End If** in addition to the **End Sub** to end the procedure. It is possible to have several End statements, one after the other. Indenting makes it easier to see which block is ended.

```
Sub Form_MouseMove (Button As Integer, Shift As Integer, ↩
   ↩x As Single, y As Single)
 If x < y Then
    BackColor = QBColor(0)
 Else
    BackColor = QBColor(5)
 End If
End Sub
```

A *Block* can be used to group statements. Use a block when there are several statements to execute when a condition is true or false:

```
If <Boolean expression> Then
  <true statement 1>
  <true statement ...>
Else
  <false statement 1>
  <false statement ...>
End If
```

The "Quadrant" Program

The "Quadrant" program changes the caption to "Top Left", "Bottom Right", etc. depending on the location of the mouse. The scalewidth and scaleheight properties of the form are used. *(If we check the properties of the form and see that it has a width of 1000, and then use the Boolean expression x<500, the program will not work if we re-size the form. By dividing the scalewidth by 2 we get the midpoint of the form even if it is re-sized.)*

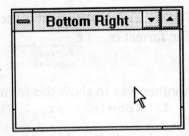

① **Start a new project** (Select **F**ile, **N**ew Project). Write the code shown below:

```
Sub Form_MouseMove (Button As Integer, Shift As Integer, ⟳
    ⟳ x As Single, y As Single)
  If y < scaleheight / 2 Then
      caption = "Top "              'give caption a new value
  Else caption = "Bottom "
  End If
  If x < scalewidth / 2 Then
      caption = caption & "Left"    'add the word left to caption
  Else
      caption = caption & "Right"
  End If
End Sub
```

Run the program: move the mouse around to see what happens. Re-size the form to see if the program still works.

② **Save the file** as B:\quadrant.frm, save the project as B:\quadrant.mak (Don't forget to remove unnecessary files first!)

Note: The programs in this chapter include some arithmetic calculations. The operators used are: plus + ; minus - ; divide / ; and multiplication * . Calculations are discussed in greater detail in Chapter 5.

ElseIF

The "Middle" Program uses an **ElseIf** statement. This program changes the caption to "Left", "Right", or "Middle" depending on the location of the mouse.
If **x** is less than 1/3 the scalewidth, the caption is "Left". Otherwise if **x** is less than 2/3 the scalewidth, the caption is "Middle". If neither of those two conditions is true, the caption is "Right".

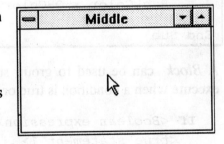

① **Start a new project** (Select **F**ile, **N**ew Project).

② **Write the code:**

```
Sub Form_MouseMove (Button As Integer, Shift As Integer, ◇
   ◇ x As Single, Y As Single)
  If x < scalewidth / 3 Then
     caption = "Left"
  ElseIf x < 2 / 3 * scalewidth Then
     caption = "Middle"
  Else
     caption = "Right"
  End If
End Sub
```

③ **Save the file** as B:\middle.frm, save the project as B:\middle.mak

Summary of IF Statements

If statements can have any of the formats below:

* One statement to execute when True:
  If *<Boolean expression>* **Then** *<statement>*

* One statement to execute when True, one when false:
  If *<Boolean expression>* **Then** *<statement>* **Else** *<statement>*

* Several statements to execute when True, none when false:
  If *<Boolean expression>* **Then**
      <statements>
  End If

* A Block: one or more statements to execute when true, one or more when false
  If *<Boolean expression>* **Then**
      <statements>
  Else
      <statements>
  End If

* If Else Group: more than one condition to test
  If *<Boolean expression1>* **Then**
      <statements>
  ElseIf *<Boolean expression2>* **Then**
      <statements>
  ElseIf *<Boolean expression3>* **Then**   *'as many ElseIf statements as needed*
      <statements>
  Else *'command to execute if none of the above conditions is met*
      <statements>   *'the else block is optional*
  End If

AND And OR

A Boolean expression can test more than one condition using AND and OR to combine two or more expressions:

> **IF** *<Boolean expression1>* **OR** *<Boolean expression2>* **THEN** *<statement>*
> The *<statement>* is executed if expression1, expression2, or <u>both</u> are true.

> **IF** *<Boolean expression1>* **AND** *<Boolean expression2>* **THEN** *<statement>*
> The *<statement>* is executed if <u>both</u> expression1 <u>and</u> expression2 are true.

Example: The caption is "No" when the mouse is in the area of the form shown shaded:

```
Sub Form_MouseMove (Button As Integer, Shift As Integer,↻
   ↻ x As Single, Y As Single)
 If x < 100 Or x > scalewidth - 100 Then
     caption = "No"
 Else caption = "Yes"
 End IF
End Sub
```

The statement can be worded with an AND for the same result:

```
Sub Form_MouseMove (Button As Integer, Shift As Integer,↻
   ↻ x As Single, Y As Single)
 If x >= 100 And x <= scalewidth - 100 Then
     caption = "Yes"
 Else caption = "No"
 End IF
End Sub
```

Exercise: Change the statements above to change the caption to "No" when the mouse is in each of the shaded areas:

1. 2. 3. 4. *Try writing each problem two ways.*

Note: Each expression must be a complete Boolean expression. The statement
   If   X< 5 Or > 100 ... is not allowed: it must be written If X<5 Or X>100 ...

The AND can be used in another way: it can be used to test a binary digit (bit). Suppose you would like to know if the Ctrl key was pressed. You do not care if Alt or Shift were pressed: You are only interested in whether Ctrl was pressed or not. The shift argument (page 16) has a value of 2 if Ctrl alone is pressed. The expression If Shift AND 2 will be true if Ctrl was pressed in any combination.

Example:

```
Sub Form_MouseDown (Button As Integer, Shift As Integer,↺
  ↺ X As Single, Y As Single)
  If Shift And 2 Then
     caption = "CTRL"
  Else caption = "NOT CTRL"
  End If
End Sub
```

Declaring Variables

The previous program used the variables received by a procedure as arguments. You can also declare variables of your own. The word **Dim** (stands for dimension) is used to declare variables. Declaring a variable reserves a place in memory to store its value. The initial value given to a variable is 0 (for numbers) or a *null* string (a string with no letters, no blanks, nothing!).

Example: `Dim curX`

Variable Names must start with a letter of the alphabet: after the first letter, it can have more letters, digits, and underscores. Blanks are not allowed. Two words can be separated by an underscore, or the second word can begin with a capital letter to make it readable: **hoursWorked** or **hourly_rate**, for example. You can not use *keywords* such as **end**, **if** or **sub** that have a special meaning in Visual Basic.

Type: In Visual Basic, all variables are *variant*, (they can contain either strings or integers or decimal numbers) unless you declare a *type*. Type can be: **Integer, Long, Double, Single, Currency** and **String** (words). (See appendix H for a complete list of the types.)

Example: If you know that a variable will only be used to store integers, you can specify the type integer when you declare it: `Dim count As Integer` If you know it will be used for words, you can declare it: `Dim answer as string`

Assigning Values to a Variable: A variable can be assigned a value with the assignment statement. The format is: *variable = newvalue*

Examples:
    The new value is a constant: `x = 5`
    The new value is another variable: `x = y`
    The new value is an expression: `x = y/3`
    It can even use its current value in the expression: `x = x + 1`
    The last statement assigns a new value to X that is one more than its current value!

Note: The statement `x = 5` is an assignment statement, this is *not* the same as **IF x = 5** , which is a Boolean expression to *compare* the two values.

Local Variables

In the program below, the variable **third** is declared inside the procedure Form_MouseMove. **Third** is local to Form_MouseMove: no other procedure can use this variable. When the procedure **Form_MouseMove** ends, the variable **third** no longer has a place in memory. This program has exactly the same result as the 'Middle" program. The only difference is that 1/3 the scalewidth is stored in the variable **third**.

```
Sub Form_MouseMove (Button As Integer, Shift As Integer, ➭
      ➭ x As Single, Y As Single)
   Dim third                 'declare the variable third
   third = scalewidth / 3    'assign a value to third
   If x < third Then         'use third
     caption = "Left"
   ElseIf x < 2 * third Then  '2*third is two-thirds
     caption = "Middle"
   Else caption = "Right"
   End If
End Sub
```

Global Variables

Variables can be made global to the form (available to all procedures of the form) by declaring them in General, Declarations: Select (general) as the object, declarations as the procedure. (*You should see the line* **Option Explicit** *in this procedure.*)

The "Line" Programs

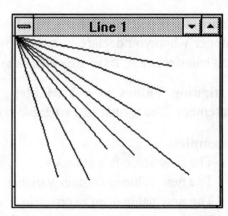

The Line programs use global variables **curX** and **curY** to draw lines. *(The **Line** procedure used in the Line programs is explained at the end of this section.)*

Line 1: Each time the mouse is clicked, a line is drawn from (X,Y) to (curX, curY). Other than the initial value of 0, curX and curY are never assigned a value. Therefore, all of the lines go into the corner (point 0,0).

① **Start a new project (Select** File, New Project**).**

② **Write the code:**

```
Option Explicit 'These two lines are in General, declarations
Dim curX, curY  'Variables declared here are global

Sub Form_MouseDown (Button As Integer, Shift As Integer, ➭
      ➭ x As Single, y As Single)
   Line (x, y)-(curX, curY)
End Sub
```

③ **Save the file** as B:\line1.frm, save the project as B:\line1.mak

Line 2: Each time the mouse is clicked, a line is drawn from (X,Y) to (curX, curY), then **curX** is assigned the value of **X**, and **curY** is assigned the value of **Y**. The first line is from the corner, because **curX** and **curY** were initially zero.

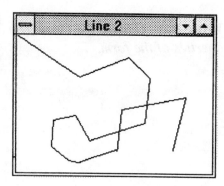

The Code for Line 2:

```
Option Explicit
Dim curX, curY

Sub Form_MouseDown (Button As Integer, Shift As Integer, ↺
   ↺ x As Single, y As Single)
   Line (x, y)-(curX, curY)
   curX = x    'curX is assigned a new value equal to the value of x
   curY = y    'curY is assigned a new value equal to the value of y
End Sub
```

Save the file as B:\line2.frm, save the project as B:\line2.mak

The "Line 3" Program

The Line 3 program assigns a value of -1 to curX in form_load. When the mouse is pressed, the mouse_down procedure first checks if the value of curX is negative: If it is, then it does not draw a line, but assigns the value of x to curX. This will happen the first time only (*no point on the form can have a negative value*). The second time the mouse is clicked, the value of curX will not be negative, so the line is drawn, then curX and curY are given the values of the current position.

①: **Modify** the code as shown below:

```
Option Explicit
Dim curX, curY

Sub Form_Load ()
   curX = -1   'no point on the form can have negative X or Y values
End Sub

Sub Form_MouseDown (Button As Integer, Shift As Integer, ↺
    ↺ x As Single, y As Single)
   If curX > 0 Then Line (x, y)-(curX, curY)
   curX = x      'make this location the current one
   curY = y
End Sub
```

② **Save the file** as B:\line3.frm, save the project as B:\line3.mak

A Little Fun: *Change the DrawStyle and/or DrawWidth properties of the form.*

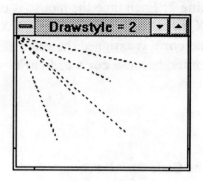

Exercise: Change the code for the line 3 program as shown below. Study the code before you run it, try to figure out what the program does. Run the program to see if you were right.

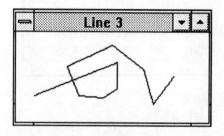

```
Sub Form_MouseDown (Button As Integer, Shift As Integer, ⬎
       ⬎ x As Single, Y As Single)
  If curX < 0 Then
     curX = x
     curY = Y
  Else
     Line (x, Y)-(curX, curY)  'draw line
     curX = -1
End If
End Sub
```

Try other variations on this program: make the line blue if shift is down, red otherwise, etc. Use your imagination to think of variations.

The Debug Window

Sometimes a program does not work the way you hoped. Suppose you added the code above and it doesn't draw any lines at all, or the lines seem to be in the wrong place. You can pause the execution and examine the values of variables in the Debug window:

① Run the program, click the pause button on the tool bar: When you finish looking at the debug window, you can press the start button to its left, or the end button to its right:

② If the Debug window does not appear, select **Window, Debug** from the menu:

③ In the Debug Window, type a question mark followed by the name of a variable. You can only check the value of global variables and properties, such as curX, scaleWidth, and variables that are local to the procedure that is currently executing.

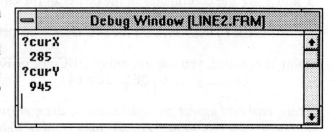

```
Debug Window [LINE2.FRM]
?curX
  285
?curY
  945
```

If you ask about the value of an unknown variable, type **?X**, for example, you will get an error message. *(Remember, local variables do not exist outside their procedure, and the MouseDown procedure could not have been executing when you clicked the pause button.)*

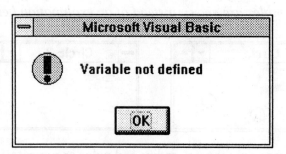

```
Microsoft Visual Basic

(!)  Variable not defined

      OK
```

Visual Basic includes a Tutorial on using other debugging tools:
- Select Help
- Select Learning Microsoft Visual Basic (not enabled if you are paused).
- Select Debugging your Application. Press the > button to watch an animated demonstration of the debug tools.

Drawing Procedures

Line: The Line Procedure has this format: *(color and box are optional)*
```
Line (<x1>,<y1>)-(<x2>,<y2>),<color>,<box>
```
    x1,y1 is the starting point of the line

    x2,y2 is the end point of the line

    color is optional, you can use either QBColor or RGB function.
```
Line(3,19)-(23,100),QBColor(5)
```
    box is optional: if you want to draw a **box** instead of a line, put a **B** here
```
Line(0,0)-(12,60),QBColor(4),B
```
     boxFilled: if you want the box to be filled in (solid), use **BF**
```
Line(5,5)-(14,50),QBColor(12),BF
```

If you want to specify Box, but no color use a comma
```
Line(5,3)-(30,20), ,B
```
Pset: The Pset procedure draws a single dot, the format is:
```
PSet(<x>,<y>),<color>
```
x and **y** are the coordinates of the points.
color is optional, you can use either QBColor or RGB function
```
PSet(5,20),RGB(255,0,0)
```

Circle: The Circle Procedure has this format:
```
Circle(<x>,<y>),<radius>,<color>,<start>,<end>,<aspect>
```

x and **y** are the coordinates of the center of the circle

radius is the radius based on the *scaleMode* property of the form.

color is optional, you can use either QBColor or RGB function.
```
circle(x,y),20,QBColor(4)
```

Start, end and aspect are used to draw, arcs, ellipses, etc. A full description of this method is in HELP! - if you're into circles, look it up in help and have fun!)
Examples are shown instead of an explanation here.

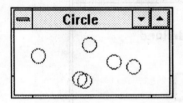
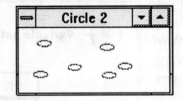
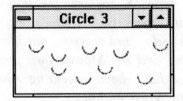

Circle uses only the x,y, radius and color arguments:
```
Circle(x,y),100,QBColor(5)
```

Circle 2 uses the *aspect* argument:
```
Circle(x,y),100,QBColor(5), , , .5
```

Circle 3 uses the *start* and *end* arguments:
```
Circle(x,y),100,QBColor(5),1*pi,2*pi
```

```
Option Explicit
Dim pi As Single 'needed because start and end must be in radians

Sub Form_Load ()
  pi = 3.14
End Sub


Sub Form_MouseDown (Button As Integer, Shift As Integer, ↳
  ↳ x As Single, y As Single)
  Circle (x, y), 100, QBColor(5), 1 * pi, 2 * pi
End Sub
```

Chapter 2

Controls

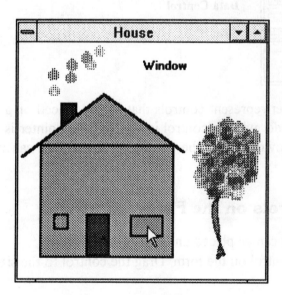

**Learn What
Controls Are**

**Use Command
Buttons**

**Use Labels to Create
"Hot Spots"**

**Use Option Buttons
for an
"International House"**

Controls on the Toolbox

When Visual Basic starts, the toolbox is on the left. The icons on the toolbox represents controls (or objects) that can be placed on the form.

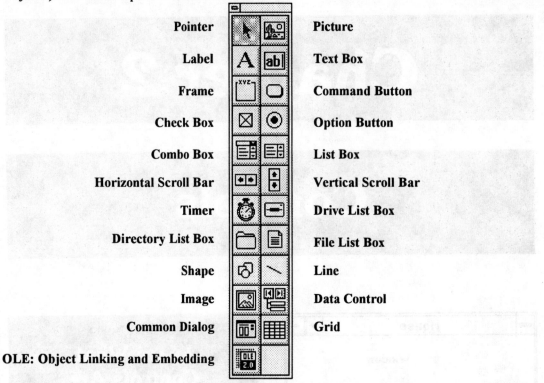

Pointer			Picture
Label			Text Box
Frame			Command Button
Check Box			Option Button
Combo Box			List Box
Horizontal Scroll Bar			Vertical Scroll Bar
Timer			Drive List Box
Directory List Box			File List Box
Shape			Line
Image			Data Control
Common Dialog			Grid
OLE: Object Linking and Embedding			

All of the icons in the toolbox except the pointer represent controls that can be placed on a form. The pointer shows the status of the design mode: when a control is selected the pointer is 'up', when no control is selected, the pointer is 'down'. When the pointer is down, you can move controls around on the form.

Placing Controls on the Form

The controls (text box, command buttons, etc.) can be placed on the form two ways:

- Double-click the control. This places the control on the form. Drag the control to the size and position desired;

- Click once on the control, then position the mouse pointer on the form: use the left mouse button to drag the control to the size desired. (This method is used to place a control inside another control, for example to place an option button inside a frame.)

Deleting a Control: You can delete a control by selecting it and pressing Delete.

Naming Controls

Visual Basic gives controls a default name: the first text box is named text1; the second text box will be text2, and so on. It is important to change the names of the controls; txtName and txtCity are easier to work with later than trying to remember that the name is in text1 and the city is text5. Change the names of controls *before* you write code for the control! It will make writing and debugging your program easier if you use a standard prefix for each type of control: txt for text boxes, lbl for labels, etc. The table below shows the suggested prefixes along with a brief description of each control. Most of these controls will be discussed in more detail later in the book - some of the controls have a whole chapter devoted to them!

Properties of the Controls

Most objects have the properties **Name, Caption, Index, Tag, Left, Width, Height, Top, BackColor, ForeColor, Visible,** and **Enabled**. If a control has text, it has **font, font size, italics** and other font properties. Properties that are unique to a particular control are shown below. A complete list of the properties of a control can be seen by placing the control on the form and looking at its properties in the property window ▣. The property window allows you to change the properties at design time. Properties can be changed at run time by statements such as `txtName.text="Hello"` , `lblInstruction.fontItalic=true`, or `hsbSize.value = 12`.

Name	Icon	Prefix	Use	Properties
Check box	⊠	chk	Any number of check boxes can be checked at one time	DataField, DataSource
Combo box		cbo	Allows user to select from a drop down list	Sorted
Command button		cmd	User selects it to execute a command	Font*, color*, Enabled, Cancel
Common Dialog			Allows common dialog boxes for color, font, and file operations at run time	
Data		dta	Connects to database to display information from database	DataBaseName, Exclusive, RecordSource
Directory list box		dir	Allows selection of directories and sub-directories	Font*, Color*
Drive list box		drv	allows selection of valid drive	Font*, Color*
File list box		fil	Allows selection from a list of files using a pattern such as *.DTA	Archive, Pattern (*.*) ReadOnly, system
Form		frm	The visible run time window	Controlbox, Icon, Picture, MDIchild
Frame		fra	Provides grouping of controls	ClipControls, Font*
Grid		grd	Allows organization of data in rows and columns	FillStyle, Cols, Rows, GridLines, GridLineWidth
Horizontal scroll bar		hsb	Allows selection of a value from a range	Max, Min, SmallChange, MousePointer
Image		img	For display of *.BMP, *.ICO and *.WMF files	Picture, Stretch
Label	A	lbl	Display only; user cannot type in this box.	Alignment, WordWrap,

Line		lin	For drawing a straight line	DrawMode, X1, X2, Y1, Y2
List box		lst	Display a list of items to select from	Columns, MultiSelect, Sorted
OLE		ole	Object linking & embedding	*Link a wordart, paint, or graph application to your program.*
Option button		opt	Only one of options in a group or frame can be selected at once	Enabled, visible, value
Picture box		pic	For display of *.BMP, *.ICO and *.WMF files or a text area	Align, ClipControls, DrawStyle, DrawWidth, fillColor, fillStyle,
Shape		shp	Add rectangle, square, oval, etc.	shape, color, fillstyle
Text box		txt	For input or display of text	DataField, DataSource, MultiLine, Scrollbars
Timer		tmr	Specify time intervals for events to occur	Interval
Vertical scroll bar		vsb	Allows selection of a value from a range	Max, Min, SmallChange, MousePointer

* Font and Color: Font* includes the properties fontSize, fontName, fontItalic, etc. Color* includes backColor and ForeColor.

The "Count" Program

① **Start a new project and design the form as shown in the illustration.**

Drag the sides of the form to approximately the size shown. Double click on the label button , then drag the label to the location and size shown. Put two command buttons on the form the same way:

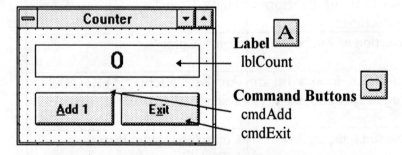

② **Change the properties (including the name property) according to the table below:**

```
Form frmCount (change the name property to frmCount)
   Caption          =    "Counter"
CommandButton cmdExit
   Caption          =    "E&xit"
CommandButton cmdAdd
   Caption          =    "&Add 1"
Label lblCount
   Alignment        =    2    'Center
   BorderStyle      =    1    'Fixed Single
   Caption          =    "0"
   FontSize         =    18
```

Note: An ampersand, **&**, in a caption makes the next letter a short-cut key. Notice the caption on the two command buttons: A̲dd 1 and E̲xit.

③ **Add code to each procedure shown below -** you only need to type the lines shown in bold.
   (The lines beginning with a quote ' are comments, a way to leave notes to yourself.)

```
Option Explicit

Sub cmdAdd_Click ()
  'Give caption a new value, 1 more than its current value:
  lblCount.Caption = lblCount.Caption + 1
End Sub

Sub cmdExit_Click ()
  'The end command is another way to stop the program
  End
End Sub
```

At run time, the user clicks the **A̲dd 1** command to increment the caption of lblCount. *(If lblCount doesn't have a caption of 0 to start, you will get an error message!)*
This command can also be executed by typing ⒜ᴸᵗ+**A**.

When finished, click the **E̲xit** command or type ⒜ᴸᵗ+**X**.
(Of course, you can still end the program the other ways you learned!)

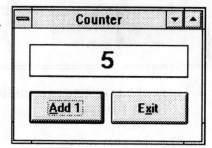

④ **Save the file** as B:\count.frm, save the project as B:\count.mak

The "House" Program

The "House" program uses labels to create "Hot Spots". When the user moves the mouse to a part of the picture a label describes the part. When the mouse moves off of the area, the label is blank.

You will need to draw a picture of a house in Windows Paint Program. Don't panic, the picture is mostly squares and lines. (the Smoke is done with "spray paint".) Appendix J gives a short introduction to the paint program if you have never used it. Save the picture as B:\HOUSE.BMP (or copy it to the clipboard and paste it on the form when you are in Visual Basic).

① **Start a New Project & Design the Form**

Put the Picture on the Form: From the property window , change the picture to B:\HOUSE.BMP by clicking on the picture property, then clicking the three dots to open the file dialog, then selecting the file. Drag the sides of the form to fit the picture.

② **Add labels** to cover each area you want to label. The labels will be white squares until you change the properties according to the table below. Drag the labels to more or less cover the area, if you want them to be more precise, you can change the left, top, height and width in the property window.

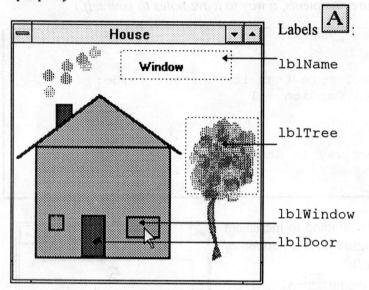

Labels [A]:

→ lblName

→ lblTree

→ lblWindow

→ lblDoor

③ **Change the properties (including the name property) according to the table below:**

```
Form frmHouse
    Caption          =    "House"
    Picture          =    B:\HOUSE.BMP
Label lblName
    Caption          =    " "
Label lblDoor
    BackStyle        =    0    'Transparent
    Caption          =    " "
Label lblWindow
    BackStyle        =    0    'Transparent
    Caption          =    " "
Label lblTree
    BackStyle        =    0    'Transparent
    Caption          =    " "
```

④ **Add code to each procedure shown below** - you only need to type the lines shown in bold:

```
Sub Form_MouseMove (Button As Integer, Shift As Integer, ↷
  ↷ X As Single, Y As Single)
 'Make the label blank when the mouse is on the form, not a label
 lblName = ""
End Sub

Sub lblDoor_MouseMove (Button As Integer, Shift As Integer, ↷
   ↷ X As Single, Y As Single)
 lblName = "Door"
End Sub
```

```
Sub lblTree_MouseMove (Button As Integer, Shift As Integer, ⇨
    ⇨ X As Single, Y As Single)
  lblName = "Tree"
End Sub

Sub lblWindow_MouseMove (Button As Integer, Shift As Integer, ⇨
    ⇨ X As Single, Y As Single)
  lblName = "Window"
End Sub
```

At run time, the user moves the mouse around to learn the parts of a house. *(OK, maybe they already know the parts of a house, but they may not know all the parts of the human body, or the countries of Africa! Try drawing those!)*

Experiment: Display additional information if the user **clicks** on a label.

⑤ **Save the file** as B:\house.frm, save the project as B:\house.mak

Control Arrays

If you add a label to the second window (the small window, to the left of the door) and change the name to lblWindow (the same name you gave the first window), you will get the message shown: Select **Yes**.
You now have a control *array*.

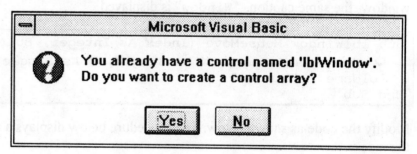

There are two labels named lblWindow, the first one, (the big window) is called `lblWindow(0)`, the second one (the small one) is `lblWindow(1)`. The number in parenthesis is called the *subscript*, or *index*. If you check the index property, you will see the index included with the object name and also in the index property. (You will need to change the backstyle and caption properties of the new label.) If you want to change a property of a *control array* at run time, you must include the index:

```
lblWindow(0).caption="Window"
```

Numbering in Visual Basic *almost* always starts with 0: Arrays start with index 0; the first color value for QBColor is 0, even the first chapter in this book is Chapter 0!

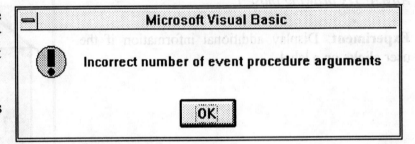

When you try to run the program, you get another error message. Visual Basic can not use the old procedure, `lblWindow_MouseMove`. It must rewrite the procedure as an array procedure.

Find the procedure `lblWindow_MouseMove` in the code view window. Highlight the line `lblName = "Window"` and copy it to the clipboard; Ctrl+X , then delete the rest of the procedure. From the object list, select `lblWindow()`. Select the `MouseMove` procedure. Paste the line `lblName = "Window"` into the procedure, Ctrl+V . The new procedure includes the index as an argument, but it is not used in this program. When the mouse moves over either window, the same caption, "`Window`" is displayed.

```
Sub lblWindow_MouseMove (Index As Integer, Button As Integer, ➮
   ➮ Shift As Integer, X As Single, Y As Single)
   lblName = "Window"
End Sub
```

Modify the code as shown below. The procedure below displays a different message depending on the index:

```
Sub lblWindow_MouseMove (index As Integer, Button As Integer, ➮
   ➮ Shift As Integer, X As Single, Y As Single)
   If index = 0 Then
     lblName.Caption = "Big Window"
   Else
     lblName = "Little Window"
     'You can leave off .Caption, it is the default!
   End If
End Sub
```

Copying Controls

When you created the control array for the window, you had to change the properties of the new control. If you use the copy command to create a control array, the properties are copied with it:

❶ Highlight lblTree by clicking on it: when it is highlighted you see black squares on the edges.

❷ Type Ctrl+C

❸ Type Ctrl+V (you will be asked if you want to create a control array, select **Yes**.

❹ The copy is in the top left corner, drag it to cover the trunk of the tree: all of the properties are the same as for the original.

You will need to change the code the same way you did when you created the control array for lblWindow.

(You can also use this method and answer **No**, to create a control with the same properties but a different name.)

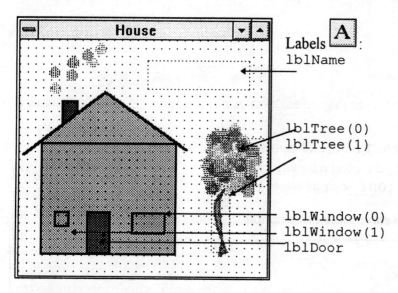

Labels A :
lblName

lblTree(0)
lblTree(1)

lblWindow(0)
lblWindow(1)
lblDoor

Experiment: Use a control array to label the roof.

The next program, the "International House" uses option buttons, the Select Case statements and uses the letters ñ and ü. These new features are explained before we begin the "International House" program.

Option Buttons ◉

Only one option button in a group can be selected. When an option button is selected a dark circle appears in the middle, the **value** property is **true**. The other option buttons in that group will have no dark circle and their **value** properties are **false**. You can change the selection at run time: `optYes.Value = True` (The value of other option buttons in the group will be automatically changed to false.)

The Case Statement

The Select Case statement is often simpler to use than an ElseIf block. The Formats are:

Single Statements:
```
Select Case <variable>
  Case <value1>: <statement1>
  Case <value2>: <statement2>
  Case Else: <statement3>    'else is optional)
End Select
```

Blocks:
```
Select Case <variable>
  Case <value1>
    <statements>
  Case value2>
    <statements>
  Case Else (optional)
    <statements>
End Select
```

`<Value>` can be a single value: `Case 1: <statement>`
A list of values: `Case 2, 4, 6, 8: <statement>`
A range of values: `Case 90 To 100: <statement>`

Examples: *(You are not expected to enter these two examples.)*

```
Select Case Ans
  Case "Y", "y"
    caption = "Yes"
    score = 1
  Case "N", "n"
    caption = "No"
    score = 3
  Case Else
    caption = "Please answer Yes or No"
End Select
```

```
Select Case Score
  Case 0 To 64: caption = "Sorry, Try Again"
  Case 65 To 80: caption = "Not Bad"
  Case Else: caption = "Very Good!"
End Select
```

Special Characters

This program uses special characters such as **ü** and **é**. To insert one of these special characters, first find its ANSI value: select <u>**H**</u>**elp**, <u>**S**</u>**earch For Help On...**, search for the word ANSI, then select ANSI Character Set. Click on the words "Characters 128-255". Scroll through the list and note the number to the left of the character you need: the letter **ü** is 252. To insert **ü** in the code hold down **Alt** and type **0252**. *(These codes are also shown in Appendix A.)*

The "International House" Program

The "International House" program uses option buttons to select a language. When the user selects a language, the title "A House" and the caption on the option buttons, "English", "Spanish" and "German" change to the language selected. The illustration shows the form after Spanish was selected.

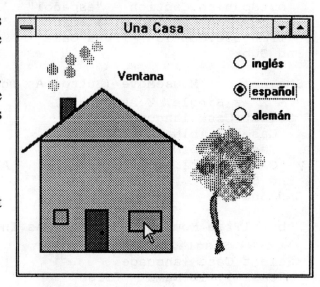

① **If it is not still open, open the "House" project.**
Save the file as `intrnat.frm` and the project as `intrnat.mak`.
(The name of the form is still frmHouse.)

② **Add three option buttons** ⊙ :
`optEnglish`, `optSpanish` and `optGerman` as shown in the illustration.

③ **Change the Properties of the option buttons, including the name, as shown below:**
```
OptionButton optGerman
    Caption        =    "German"
OptionButton optSpanish
    Caption        =    "Spanish"
OptionButton optEnglish
    Caption        =    "English"
    Value          =    true
```

Note: Several of the procedures in the next section are similar. This is a good time to try using cut and paste to save some typing!

④ **Enter the Code:** The code for Form_MouseMove is not changed. It is not shown here.

```
Option Explicit
Dim language   'English=1; Spanish=2; German=3

Sub optEnglish_click ()   'assign 1 to language, change captions
    language = 1
    optEnglish.Caption = "English"
    optSpanish.Caption = "Spanish"
    optGerman.Caption = "German"
    frmHouse.Caption = "A House"
End Sub
```

```
Sub optGerman_Click () 'assign 3 to language, change captions
  language = 3
  optEnglish.Caption = "Englisch"
  optSpanish.Caption = "Spanisch"
  optGerman.Caption = "Deutsch"
  frmHouse.Caption = "Ein Haus"
End Sub

Sub optSpanish_Click () 'assign 2 to language, change captions
  language = 2
  optEnglish.Caption = "inglés"    'ALT-0233
  optSpanish.Caption = "español"   'ALT-0241
  optGerman.Caption = "alemán"     'ALT-0225
  frmHouse.Caption = "Una Casa"
End Sub

Sub lblDoor_MouseMove (Button As Integer, Shift As Integer, ⇨
  ⇨X As Single, Y As Single)
 Select Case language
   Case 1: lblName = "Door"
   Case 2: lblName = "Puerta"
   Case 3: lblName = "Tür"        'ALT-0252
 End Select
End Sub

Sub lblTree_MouseMove (Button As Integer, Shift As Integer, ⇨
  ⇨X As Single, Y As Single)
 Select Case language
   Case 1: lblName = "Tree"
   Case 2: lblName = "Arbol"
   Case 3: lblName = "Baum"
 End Select
End Sub

Sub lblWindow_MouseMove (Button As Integer, Shift As Integer, ⇨
  ⇨X As Single, Y As Single)
 Select Case language
   Case 1: lblName = "Window"
   Case 2: lblName = "Ventana"
   Case 3: lblName = "Fenster"
 End Select
End Sub
```

⑤ **Save the project. (It has already been named.)**

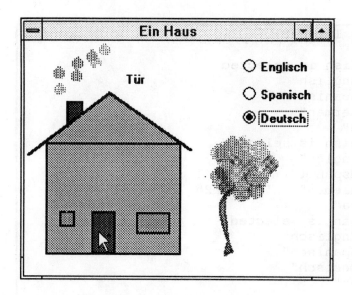

The "International House" Program 2: An Array of Option Buttons

The International House program is modified to use a control array for the option buttons.

① **Rename the option buttons as `optLanguage`.** Answer Yes when asked if you want to create a control array.

> `optLanguage(0)` is English, `(1)` is Spanish and `(2)` is German.

The global variable language is omitted. There is only one `optLanguage_Click` procedure - it uses the index and a select case statement to change the captions.

② **Modify the code as shown below:**

```
Sub lblDoor_MouseMove (Button As Integer, Shift As Integer, ↺
    ↺ X As Single, Y As Single)
  If optLanguage(0).Value = True Then lblName = "Door"
  If optLanguage(1).Value = True Then lblName = "Puerta"
  If optLanguage(2).Value = True Then lblName = "Tür"
End Sub

Sub lblTree_MouseMove (Button As Integer, Shift As Integer, ↺
    ↺X As Single, Y As Single)
  If optLanguage(0).Value = True Then lblName = "Tree"
  If optLanguage(1).Value = True Then lblName = "Arbol"
  If optLanguage(2).Value = True Then lblName = "Baum"
End Sub

Sub lblWindow_MouseMove (Button As Integer, Shift As Integer, ↺
    ↺ X As Single, Y As Single)
  If optLanguage(0).Value = True Then lblName = "Window"
  If optLanguage(1).Value = True Then lblName = "Ventana"
  If optLanguage(2).Value = True Then lblName = "Fenster"
End Sub
```

```
Sub optLanguage_click (index As Integer)
  Select Case index
  Case 0   'index is 0 when English is selected
    optLanguage(0).Caption = "English"
    optLanguage(1).Caption = "Spanish"
    optLanguage(2).Caption = "German"
    frmHouse.Caption = "A House"
  Case 1   'index is 1 when Spanish is selected
    optLanguage(0).Caption = "inglés"     'ALT-0233
    optLanguage(1).Caption = "español"    'ALT-0241
    optLanguage(2).Caption = "alemán"     'ALT-0225
    frmHouse.Caption = "Una Casa"
  Case 2   'index is 2 when German is selected
    optLanguage(0).Caption = "Englisch"
    optLanguage(1).Caption = "Spanisch"
    optLanguage(2).Caption = "Deutsch"
    frmHouse.Caption = "Ein Haus"
  End Select
End Sub
```

When you try to run it you will get an error message: you need to delete all of the code for optEnglish, optSpanish and optGerman because those option buttons no longer exist.

③ **Save the project.**

Chapter 3

The Users Choice

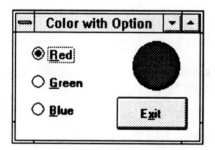

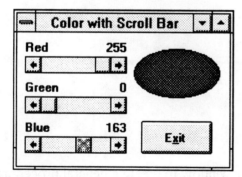

**Create a
General Procedure**

**Compare
Check Boxes
&
Option Buttons**

Use Scroll Bars

General Procedures

In the previous chapters, all of the procedures that you wrote code for were events for a specific object. In the "Color Option" program, the same set of instructions need to be executed for several procedures. Instead of having several procedures that do the same thing, we will write a General Procedure and then call that procedure when we need it.

The "Color Option" Program

This program uses option buttons to select colors. The user can select one of the option buttons to change the color of the shape.

① **Start a new project and build the form as shown below:**

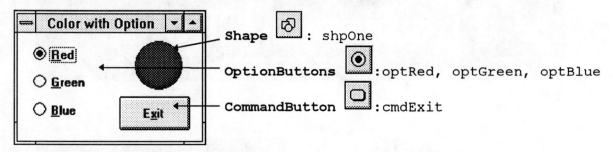

② **Change the Properties (including the name):**

```
Form  frmColor1              (select an icon of your choice)
  Caption           =     "Color with Option"
CommandButton cmdExit
  Caption           =     "E&xit"

OptionButton optRed
  Caption           =     "&Red"
OptionButton optGreen
  Caption           =     "&Green"
OptionButton optBlue
  Caption           =     "&Blue"
Shape shpOne
  FillStyle         =     0    'Solid
  Shape             =     3    'Circle
```

Create a General Procedure: You must be in a code window to create a general procedure. If you are on the form, you can double-click to open a code window.

③ **From a Code window, select from the menu bar View, New Procedure**

The New Procedure dialog window opens. The default type is **Sub**routine, and it is already selected. Type the name of the procedure, then select OK. (OK is disabled until you type a name.) Name the procedure `colorOption`.

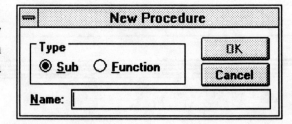

④ A procedure window with the name you typed opens. Enter the code shown below, then enter the code for the rest of the procedures.

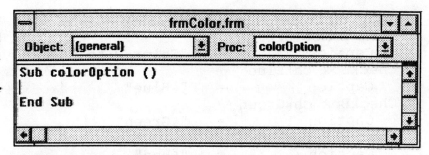

```
Sub colorOption () 'Assigns values to local var. for RGB values
Dim Red, Green, Blue
  If optRed.Value = True Then Red = 255 Else Red = 0
  If optGreen.Value = True Then Green = 255 Else Green = 0
  If optBlue.Value = True Then Blue = 255 Else Blue = 0
  shpOne.FillColor = RGB(Red, Green, Blue)
End Sub

Sub cmdExit_Click () 'End execution
  End
End Sub

Sub optRed_Click ()
  colorOption  'call the procedure colorOption
End Sub

Sub optGreen_Click ()
  colorOption  'call the procedure colorOption
End Sub

Sub optBlue_Click ()
  colorOption  'call the procedure colorOption
End Sub
```

⑤ **Save the file** as B:\clr_opt.frm, save the project as B:\clr_opt.mak

The "Color Check" Program

This is very similar to the Color Option Program, except that it uses Check Boxes instead of option buttons.

① **Start a new project and design the Form:**

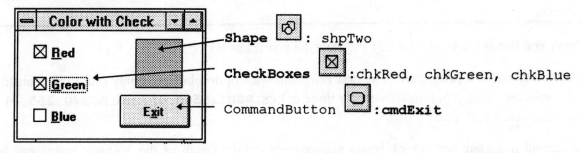

② **Change the Properties** (including the name):

```
Form frmColor2
    Caption              =    "Color with Check"
CheckBox chkBlue
    Caption              =    "&Blue"
CheckBox chkGreen
    Caption              =    "&Green"
CheckBox chkRed
    Caption              =    "&Red"
CommandButton cmdExit
    Caption              =    "E&xit"
Shape shpTwo
    FillStyle            =    0    'Solid
    Shape                =    1    'Square
```

③ **Create a General Procedure named colorCheck** (see if you can do it without looking at the instructions)

```
Sub colorCheck ()
Dim Red, Green, Blue
  If chkRed.Value = 1 Then Red = 255 Else Red = 0
  If chkGreen.Value = 1 Then Green = 255 Else Green = 0
  If chkBlue.Value = 1 Then Blue = 255 Else Blue = 0
  shpTwo.FillColor = RGB(Red, Green, Blue)
End Sub
```

④ **Add the Rest of the Code:**

```
Sub chkRed_Click ()
  colorCheck
End Sub

Sub chkGreen_Click ()
  colorCheck
End Sub

Sub chkBlue_Click ()
  colorCheck
End Sub

Sub cmdExit_Click ()
  End
End Sub
```

⑤ **Save the file** as `B:\clr_chk.frm`, save the project as `B:\clr_chk.mak`

Compare these two programs: The first program, with option buttons, only one option button can be selected. This program allows only three colors: `RGB(255,0,0)`, red; `RGB(0,255,0)`, green, and `RGB(0,0,255)`, blue.

The second program, with check boxes allows eight colors: (each of the 3 check boxes can be checked or unchecked: 2*2*2=8): `RGB(0,0,0)`, `RGB(0,0,255)`, `RGB(0,255,0)`, `RGB(0,255,255)`, `RGB(255,0,0)`, `RGB(255,0,255)`, `RGB(255,255,0)`, and `RGB(255,255,255)`.

The "QBColor" Program

The "QBColor" program uses a scroll bar to select a number from 0 to 15. The number selected is used to change the fillcolor property of a shape.

Scroll Bars

The horizontal scroll bar [image], and the vertical scroll bar [image] have the same properties and events, use whichever you prefer.

Parts of the scroll bar:

←Decrease: Each click decreases the value by 1. (The left button on a horizontal scroll bar)

←Thumb: press down on left mouse button and drag up and down or left and right.

←Increase: Each click increases the value by 1. (The right button on a horizontal scroll bar)

The procedure **Change** is executed when the user clicks on the increase or decrease buttons, or *releases* the left mouse button after using the thumb. The procedure **Scroll** is executed whenever the user moves the thumb. Most of the time, you will want to execute the same instructions in **Scroll** and **Change**. To execute the same code for both events, you can use one of the following methods:

- Use the same code in both places. (Type the code in the **Change** procedure, then use Copy and paste to insert the code in the **Scroll** procedure.)

- Put the code in one procedure and call that procedure from the other procedure.

- Use a general procedure: both **Change** and **Scroll** call the general procedure.

① **Start a new project and design the form:**

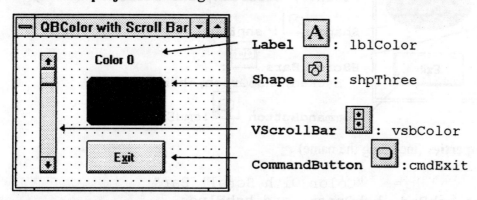

② **Change the Properties** (including the name):

```
Form frmColor3
    Caption         =     "QBColor with Scroll Bar"
CommandButton cmdExit
    Caption         =     "E&xit"
```

```
VScrollBar vsbColor
   Max                    =     15
   Min                    =      0
Label lblColor
   Caption                =    "Color 0"
Shape shpThree
   FillStyle              =     0   'Solid
   Shape                  =     4   'Rounded Rectangle
```

③ **Write The Code for the QBColor Scroll Bar Program:**

```
Sub cmdExit_Click () 'End the program
   End
End Sub

Sub vsbColor_Change () 'Use the value property of the scroll bar
   lblColor.Caption = "Color " & vsbColor.Value
   shpThree.FillColor = QBColor(vsbColor.Value)
End Sub
```

④ **Save the file** as B:\clr_qb1.frm, save the project as B:\clr_qb1.mak

The "RGBColor" Program

The "RGBColor" program uses three Scroll Bars to select the red, green and blue values. Many more colors are available with this program if your monitor can display them.

① **Start a new project and design the form:**

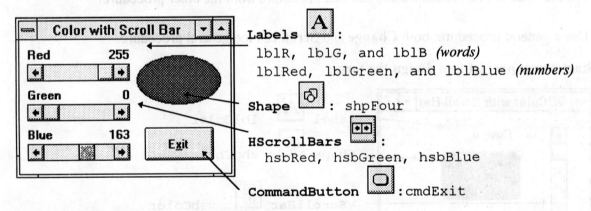

Labels [A] :
   lblR, lblG, and lblB *(words)*
   lblRed, lblGreen, and lblBlue *(numbers)*

Shape : shpFour

HScrollBars :
   hsbRed, hsbGreen, hsbBlue

CommandButton :cmdExit

② **Change the Properties** (including the name):

```
Form frmColor4
   Caption                =    "Color with Scroll Bar"
HScrollBars hsbRed, hsbGreen, and hsbBlue:
   Max                    =    255
   Min                    =      0
CommandButton cmdExit
   Caption                =    "E&xit"
```

```
Label lblRed, lblGreen, and lblBlue
  Alignment          =    1   'Right Justify
  Caption            =    "0"
Label LabelR
  Caption            =    "Red"
Label LabelG
  Caption            =    "Green"
Label LabelB
  Caption            =    "Blue"
Shape shpFour
  FillStyle          =    0   'Solid
  Shape              =    2   'Oval
```

③ **Write the code for the "RGB Color" Program:**

```
Sub cmdExit_Click () 'End the program
  End
End Sub

Sub colorScroll ()   'A General Procedure
Dim Red, Green, Blue
  Red = hsbRed.Value
  Green = hsbGreen.Value
  Blue = hsbBlue.Value
  shpFour.FillColor = RGB(Red, Green, Blue)
End Sub

'For hsbBlue the same code is repeated in scroll and change
Sub hsbBlue_Change ()
  lblBlue.Caption = hsbBlue.Value
  colorScroll
End Sub

Sub hsbBlue_Scroll ()
  lblBlue.Caption = hsbBlue.Value
  colorScroll
End Sub

'For hsbGreen the code is in scroll; and change calls scroll
Sub hsbGreen_Change ()
  hsbGreen_scroll     'call the procedure hsb_Scroll
End Sub

Sub hsbGreen_scroll ()
  lblGreen.Caption = hsbGreen.Value
  colorScroll
End Sub

Sub hsbRed_Change ()
  lblRed.Caption = hsbRed.Value
  colorScroll
End Sub
```

```
Sub hsbRed_Scroll ()
  hsbRed_Change
End Sub
```

④ **Save the file** as B:\clr_rgb.frm, save the project as B:\clr_rgb.mak

The "Color 5" Program

The Fifth Color Program uses an array of option buttons to select a QBColor. The QBColor is used to change the fillcolor property of shape five. This program changes the captions of the option buttons during form_load instead of at design time.

① **Start a new project,** (Select **File**, **New Project**)

② **Design the form**: Place an option button on the form: change the name property to **optColor**. Change the width to 1580 and the height to 255. Copy optColor, ⌷Ctrl⌷+**C**, then paste ⌷Ctrl⌷+**V**. (Answer **Yes** to create a control array.) Drag the new control into position. Repeat until you have 16 option buttons. (They are numbered optColor(0), optColor(1) ... optColor(15). Leave the caption alone.

③ **Save the file** as B:\clr_qb2.frm, save the project as B:\clr_qb2.mak

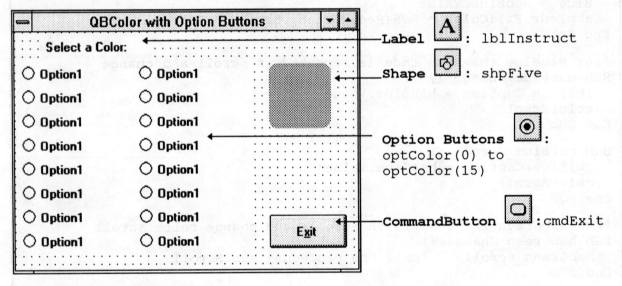

④ **Change the Properties:**
```
Form frmColor5
     Caption          =      "QBColor with Option Buttons"
CommandButton cmdExit
     Caption          =      "E&xit"
Shape shpFive
     FillStyle        =      0    'Solid
     Shape            =      5    'Rounded Square
Label lblInstruct
     Caption          =      "Select a Color:"
```

⑤ **Add the Code for Color 5**

```
Sub cmdExit_Click () 'End the program
  End
End Sub

Sub optColor_Click (index As Integer) 'Use Index as the QBColor
  shpFive.FillColor = QBColor(index)
End Sub
Sub Form_Load () 'Change the captions at run time
  optColor(0).Caption = "Black"
  optColor(1).Caption = "Blue"
  optColor(2).Caption = "Green"
  optColor(3).Caption = "Cyan"
  optColor(4).Caption = "Red"
  optColor(5).Caption = "Magenta"
  optColor(6).Caption = "Yellow"
  optColor(7).Caption = "White"
  optColor(8).Caption = "Gray"
  optColor(9).Caption = "Light Blue"
  optColor(10).Caption = "Light Green"
  optColor(11).Caption = "Light Cyan"
  optColor(12).Caption = "Light Red"
  optColor(13).Caption = "Light Magenta"
  optColor(14).Caption = "Light Yellow"
  optColor(15).Caption = "Bright White"
End Sub
```

⑥ **Save the file** (It has already been named `clr_qb2.frm` and `clr_qb2.mak`.)

When the program is running, the user sees the names of the colors.

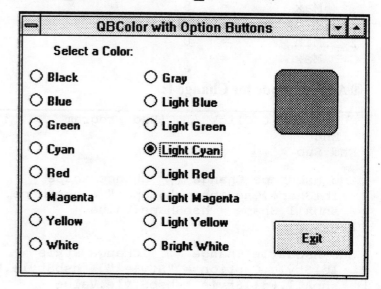

The "Change" Program

The next program uses two scroll bars: the first changes the shape of shpAll, the second changes the fillStyle property. At run time, the user can use the scroll bar to select shape and fill style. You can add scroll bars to change other properties.

① **Start a new project**, (Select **File**, **New Project**).

② **Design the form**:

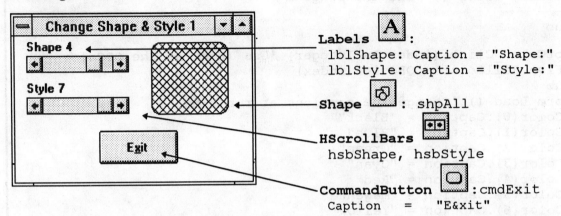

③ **Change the Properties**: Before you change the properties of the scroll bars, look at the property list for **shpAll**: click on **fillStyle** and pull down the list of choices: ⬇ note that the list has choices from 0 to 7: **hsbStyle** will have a **min** of 0 and a **max** of 7. When you check the shape property, you will see that the choices are numbered 0 to 5: those are the **min** and **max** values for **hsbShape**. (Don't forget to change the names!)

```
Form frmChange1
   Caption    = "Change Shape & Style 1"
HScrollBar hsbShape
   Min        =    0
   Max        =    5
HScrollBar hsbStyle
   Min        =    0
   Max        =    7
```

⑤ **Add the Code for Change 1**:

```
Sub cmdExit_Click ()    'End program
  End
End Sub

Sub hsbShape_Change () 'Change shape
  lblShape.Caption = "Shape " & hsbShape.Value
  shpAll.Shape = hsbShape.Value
End Sub

Sub hsbStyle_Change ()   'Change style
  lblStyle.Caption = "Style " & hsbStyle.Value
  shpAll.FillStyle = hsbStyle.Value
End Sub
```

⑥ **Save the file** as B:\change1.frm, **save the project** as B:\change1.mak

Chapter 4

Groups of Choices

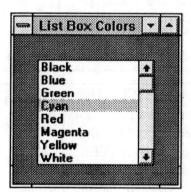

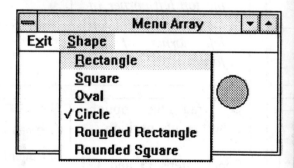

**Use Frames
to Group
Option Buttons**

Use a List Box

Create a Menu

**Create a
Menu Array**

Frames

In the last chapter, the "Change" program used two scroll bars to select the FillStyle and shape properties of a shape control. If you want to write the same program using option buttons, you must use frames to create two groups of option buttons.

The "Change 2" Program

Two groups of option buttons are used to select the *shape* and the *fillStyle* of a shape. Only one option button in a group can be selected. Option buttons can be made into separate groups by placing the option buttons in a frame. One option button in each frame can be selected.

① **Start a new project and build the form:**

② **Follow the steps below** to place the **optShape** buttons inside a frame:

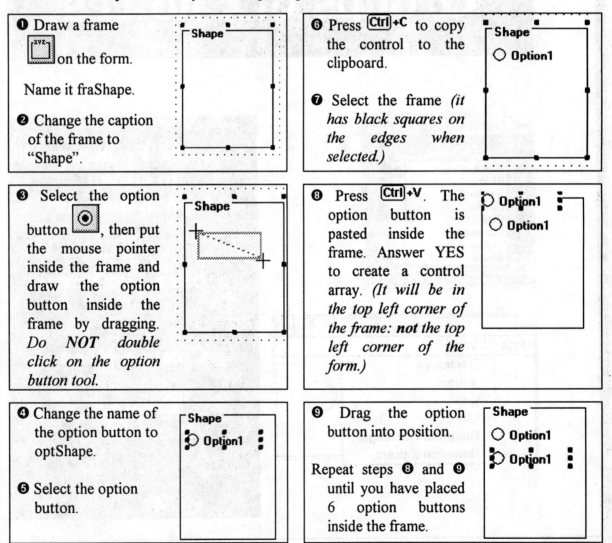

❶ Draw a frame on the form.

Name it fraShape.

❷ Change the caption of the frame to "Shape".

❸ Select the option button , then put the mouse pointer inside the frame and draw the option button inside the frame by dragging. *Do **NOT** double click on the option button tool.*

❹ Change the name of the option button to optShape.

❺ Select the option button.

❻ Press Ctrl+C to copy the control to the clipboard.

❼ Select the frame *(it has black squares on the edges when selected.)*

❽ Press Ctrl+V. The option button is pasted inside the frame. Answer YES to create a control array. *(It will be in the top left corner of the frame: **not** the top left corner of the form.)*

❾ Drag the option button into position.

Repeat steps ❽ and ❾ until you have placed 6 option buttons inside the frame.

③ **Create a Frame for the "Style" Option Buttons**: Follow the same steps to create a frame fraStyle that contains 8 option buttons named **optStyle**. The completed form is shown on the next page.

The Completed Form for the "Frames Program":

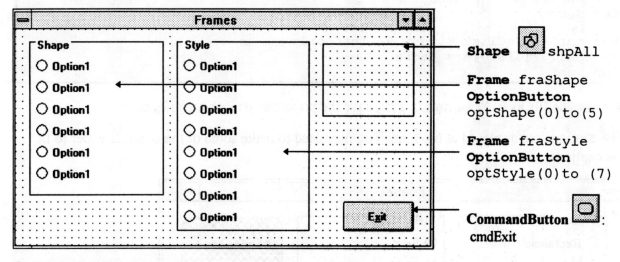

④ **Change the following properties:**

```
Form frmFrames
   Caption          =    "Frames"
CommandButton cmdExit
   Caption          =    "E&xit"
Frame fraStyle: Containing OptionButton optStyle(0) to(7)
   Caption          =    "Style"
Frame fraShape: Containing OptionButton optShape(0) to (5)
   Caption          =    "Shape"
Shape shpAll       (no properties need to be changed)
```

⑤ **Add the code:**

```
Sub cmdExit_Click ()    'End program
   End
End Sub

Sub Form_Load () 'Change captions at run time
   optStyle(0).Caption = "Solid"
   optStyle(1).Caption = "Transparent"
   optStyle(2).Caption = "Horizontal Lines"
   optStyle(3).Caption = "Vertical Lines"
   optStyle(4).Caption = "Upward Diagonal"
   optStyle(5).Caption = "Downward Diagonal"
   optStyle(6).Caption = "Cross"
   optStyle(7).Caption = "Diagonal Cross"
   optShape(0).Caption = "Rectangle"
   optShape(1).Caption = "Square"
   optShape(2).Caption = "Oval"
   optShape(3).Caption = "Circle"
   optShape(4).Caption = "Rounded Rectangle"
   optShape(5).Caption = "Rounded Square"
End Sub
```

```
Sub optShape_Click (index As Integer)
  shpAll.Shape = index
End Sub

Sub optStyle_Click (index As Integer)
  shpAll.FillStyle = index
End Sub
```

⑥ **Save the file** as B:\change2.frm, save the project as B:\change2.mak

The captions are displayed at run time: You may need to make some of the controls wider to fit the captions.

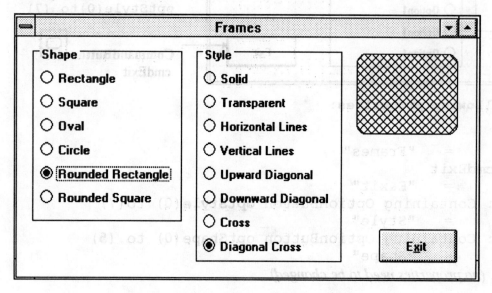

List Boxes

A list box is another way to group a list of choices. In the "List Box Colors" program, The names of the 16 QBColors are loaded into the list box at form load. When a color is selected from the list box, its listIndex property is used to change the background color of the form. (Listindex is an items position in the list - the first item added to the list has a listindex of 0, the next item added has a listindex of 1, etc.

① **Start a new project and build the form:**

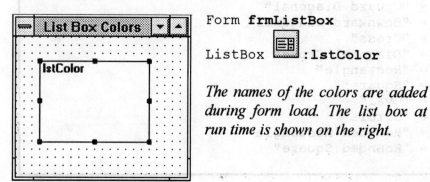

Form **frmListBox**

ListBox : **lstColor**

The names of the colors are added during form load. The list box at run time is shown on the right.

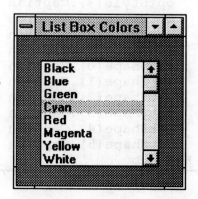

② **Change the names and properties:**

Form **frmListBox**   Caption = "List Box Colors"
ListBox:**lstColor**   *(stretch to fit list after running once)*

③ **Write the Code:**

```
Sub Form_Load () 'Names of colors are added in order:
   lstColor.AddItem "Black"    ' ListIndex is 0
   lstColor.AddItem "Blue"     ' ListIndex is 1
   lstColor.AddItem "Green"    ' ListIndex is 2, etc.
   lstColor.AddItem "Cyan"     ' The ListIndex for the selected item
   lstColor.AddItem "Red"      ' is passed to the QBColor procedure
   lstColor.AddItem "Magenta"  ' when a color is selected from list
   lstColor.AddItem "Yellow"
   lstColor.AddItem "White"
   lstColor.AddItem "Gray"
   lstColor.AddItem "Light Blue"
   lstColor.AddItem "Light Green"
   lstColor.AddItem "Light Cyan"
   lstColor.AddItem "Light Red"
   lstColor.AddItem "Light Magenta"
   lstColor.AddItem "Light Yellow"
   lstColor.AddItem "Bright White"
End Sub

Sub lstColor_Click ()
'When a color is selected, background color is changed
   frmListBox.BackColor = QBColor(lstColor.ListIndex)
End Sub
```

④ **Save the file** as B:\clr_list.frm, save the project as B:\clr_list.mak

Menus

A form that is covered with frames and option buttons starts to get *very* crowded! Menus allow you to move the users choices off of the form. The program below does exactly the same thing as the previous program, but uses a menu instead of frames. The running program shows a menu bar. The main menu will show **Exit**, **Shape** and **Style**.

Clicking **Shape** gives you a sub-menu with the choices:
```
   Rectangle
   Square
   Oval
```

Clicking **Style** gives you a sub-menu with the choices
```
   Solid
   Transparent
   Horizontal lines
```
(You can add the other choices later.)

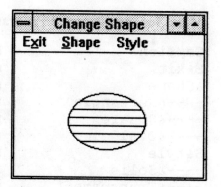

① **Start a new project.**

② **Build the menu**: Press the menu design icon on the **toolbar**: 🗒 *(Don't confuse this with the combo box* 🗒 *on the toolbox.)* The menu design window appears as shown on right. Type **E&xit** in caption, then press **Tab** to move the cursor to name. Type **mnuExit** as name. Press **⏎Enter**

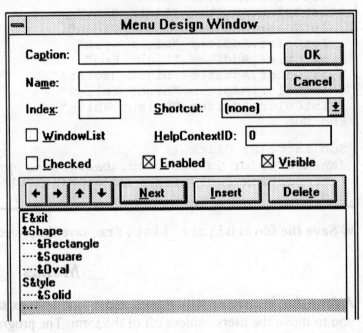

Add the second menu item, **Shape** the same way: Type **&Shape** in caption, Press **Tab** to move the cursor to name: Type **mnuShape,** as name, then Press **⏎Enter**.

The menu design Window now has two entries. The next entry, **Rectangle**, is in the sub-menu for **Shape.** Before you type the caption, press **➡**. You will see ---- below **&Shape**; this indicates a sub-menu. Enter the caption and name for rectangle from the table below. When you press **⏎Enter**, the ---- appears for the next entry. Enter each caption and name as shown in the table and in the illustration. When you finish entering the shapes, press **⬅** to go back to the top level before you enter **S&tyle**, then press **➡** again to indent for the **style** sub-menu.

When all of the items have been entered, press OK.

Menu for the Change 3 Program:

Caption	Name
E&xit	mnuExit
&Shape	mnuShape
----&Rectangle	mnuRectangle
----&Square	mnuSquare
----&Oval	mnuOval
S&tyle	mnuStyle
----&Solid	mnuSolid
----&Transparent	mnuTransparent
----&Horizontal Lines	mnuHorizontal

③ **Build the Form and Change the Names of the Controls:**

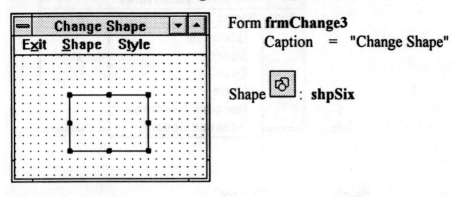

Form **frmChange3**
   Caption   =   "Change Shape"

Shape : **shpSix**

④ **Add the Code:**

```
Sub mnuExit_Click ()
  End
End Sub

Sub mnuRectangle_Click ()
  shpSix.Shape = 0
End

Sub mnuSquare_Click ()
  shpSix.Shape = 1
End Sub

Sub mnuOval_Click ()
  shpSix.Shape = 2
End Sub

Sub mnuSolid_Click ()
  shpSix.FillStyle = 0
End Sub

Sub mnuTransparent_Click ()
  shpSix.FillStyle = 1
End Sub

Sub mnuHorizontal_Click ()
  shpSix.FillStyle = 2
End Sub
```

⑤ **Save the file** as B:\change3.frm, save the project as B:\change3.mak

Menu Arrays

Menu items can be arrays. This is a variation on the previous program: only the **Shape** is selected. You can create the **Style** selection in the same way. When you create a menu array you must assign an index. The indices of a menu array must be in ascending order, but numbers can be skipped. *(For example, you could leave out Oval and Circle in the example below.)*

Start a new project and build the Form:

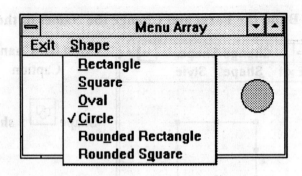

```
Form frmMenu
    Caption  = "Menu Array"

Shape       shpSix
    FillStyle = 0 'Solid
```

The current selection is checked ✓ at run time.

The menu:

Caption	Name	Index
E&xit	mnuExit	
&Shape	mnuShapeHdr	
----&Rectangle	mnuShape	0
----&Square	mnuShape	1
----&Oval	mnuShape	2
----&Circle	mnuShape	3
----Rou&nded Rectangle	mnuShape	4

The Code:

```
Sub mnuExit_Click () 'End the program
    End
End

Sub mnuShape_Click (index As Integer) 'Index is an argument
    shpSix.Shape = index              'Change the shape
    'Uncheck all of the choices, then check the selected one
    'That is easier than using an IF Else to find the one selected
    mnuShape(0).Checked = False
    mnuShape(1).Checked = False
    mnuShape(2).Checked = False
    mnuShape(3).Checked = False
    mnuShape(4).Checked = False
mnuShape(index).Checked = True    'Check the current selection
End Sub
```

⑤ **Save the file** as B:\change4.frm, save the project as B:\change4.mak

Note: There is an easier way to uncheck all of the choices using a **For Loop**:

```
Sub mnuShape_Click (index As Integer)
Dim s
    shpSix.Shape = index              'Change the shape
    For s = 0 To 4
        mnuShape(s).Checked = False    'Uncheck all
    Next s
    mnuShape(index).Checked = True    'Check the current selection
End Sub
```

This is a preview: For Loops are discussed in chapter 6!

Chapter 5

Calculations

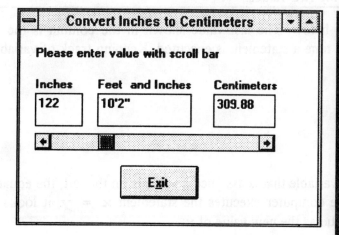

Learn to Do Arithmetic Operations

Write the "Grade" Program

Convert Inches to Centimeters

Write a Function

Arithmetic Operations

Arithmetic operations, or calculations, are an important part of programming. Almost every program includes at least a few arithmetic operations. There was a brief introduction to the assignment statement in chapter 4:

Assigning Values to a Variable

A variable can be assigned a value with the assignment statement. The format is:
   <variable> = *<newvalue>*

Examples:
   The new value is a constant: X = 5
   The new value is another variable: X = Y
   The new value is an expression: X = Y/3
   It can even use its current value in the expression: X = X + 1
   The last statement assigns a new value to X that is one more than its current value!

Note: The statement X = 5 is an assignment statement, this is *not* the same as **If** X = 5 , which is a Boolean expression to *compare* the two values.

A sequence of statements is shown below. The last value shown in the column is the current value, the current value is used each time a statement is executed. Keeping track of variables this way is called *tracing*:

Statement:	**X**
X = 5	5
X = X + 1	6
X = X + 1	7

It is important to remember that the variable that is assigned a value is on the left; the equation, or new value, is on the right: when the computer executes the statement x = y, it looks up the current value of y and stores that value as the new value of x:

Statement:	**X**	**Y**
X = 5	5	
Y = 12		12
X = Y	12	

The statement **Y = X** is *not* the same:

Statement:	**x**	**y**
X = 5	5	
Y = 12		12
Y = X		5

Check Your Answers

You can try all of the examples and problems in this section by declaring X, Y and Z as global variables, then try the problems in the debug window:

In the code view window, select in (general), declarations and declare the variables:

```
Option Explicit
Dim X, Y, Z
```

Run the program, and press the pause button
▐▐ . If the debug window doesn't appear
Select **W**indow, **D**ebug

In the debug window, you can assign values, then see the values with the question mark.

Debug Window [Form1.frm]
```
x=5
y=x
?y
 5
```

Exercise: Trace the value of each variable after executing each statement: Use the most recent value in each column: Check your answers as shown above.

Statement: **X**   **Y**
```
X = 3
Y = X
X  =  X + 2
X = Y + 1
```

Arithmetic Operators

Visual Basic has the following operators:

Operator	Purpose:	Example:	X
+	Addition	X= 5+3	8
–	Minus	X= 8-2	6
	(using most recent value of x)	X= X-1	5
*	Multiplication	X= 6*2	12
/	Division	X= 17/5	
		X= 15/5	3.5
			3
mod	Remainder	X= 17 MOD 5	2
^	Raise to a power: 4^2 is	X= 4^2	16
	4^2, 2^3 is 2^3	X= 2^3	8

An actual program would not use a statement such as X=5+3, it would save time to simply use X=8. An actual program would be more likely to use variables: X=Y+Z, for example.

Note that there is a _times_, or _multiplication_, operator: * . In algebra, variables are always a single letter, XY in algebra means X times Y. In programming, variables can be several letters, and we could not be sure whether XY meant X times Y or a variable called XY.

MOD

The mod (modulus) operator is used to find the remainder. Before children learn about decimal numbers, they may give the answer to division problems as:

"17 divided by 5 is 3 with a **remainder of 2**"

$$\begin{array}{r} 3 \\ 5\overline{\smash{)}17} \\ \underline{15} \\ 2 \leftarrow \text{17 mod 5} \end{array}$$

Note that **17/5** results in **3.5**, while **17 mod 5** results in 2.

Study tip: After studying the examples, try evaluating the expressions without looking at the answers; then do the exercise. You can check your answers using the debug window.

Exercise: Show the value of z after executing each statement:

Statement:	X	Y	Z
X = 8	8		
Y = 5		5	
Z = X+Y			
Z = X^2			
Z = X*2			
Z = X/2			
Z = X MOD 2			
Z = X-Y			
Z = Y MOD 3			

Functions

In addition to the operators shown above, Visual Basic has functions to find square root; trigonometric functions such as sin and cosine; and many others. Functions receive values and return a result: for instance **sqr(16)** will return **4**. (The *square root* of 16). **int(5.8)** will return **5**. (*int* stands for *integer*.)

If you are interested in learning more about the math functions that are available, select **Help**, **Search for Help on...** then type the word **math**. Select **math functions** and browse through the list. *(A list of built-in functions is also in Appendix E, page 181.)*

Order of Operations

A statement can perform more than one arithmetic operation. If there is more than one arithmetic operation in a statement, they are executed according to the level of the operators: Parenthesis take precedence over all other operators; multiplication and division take precedence over mod, mod takes precedence over addition and subtraction.

Evaluate an expression in the following order:

1. Anything inside parenthesis, including functions, are done first: working from the inner-most parenthesis out;

2. Raise to a power: ^ is performed from left to right;

3. Multiplication and division (*, /) are performed from left to right;

4. Mod is performed from left to right;

5. Addition and subtraction (+ and -), are performed from left to right.

Examples: The order of evaluation is shown by underlining the next operation, then replacing it with the result (in bold) on the next line.

A. 3 + 5 * 2   ** takes precedence over +*

    3 + **10**   *5*2=10: the 10 replaces 5*2 on this line*

       13   *3+10=3: the 13 replaces 3+10 on this line: Done!*

B. (3 + 5) * 2   *parenthesis first*

       8 * 2

          16   *Notice the difference between the first and second problems!*

C. 3 * (5 - 3 * 8 + 4)   *parenthesis first, within parenthesis, * before + or -*

    3 * (5 - **24** + 4)   *if same level (+ and -), work from left to right*

    3 * (**-19** + 4)

    3 * **-15**

       -45

D. 3 * (5 - 3) * (8 + 4)   *parenthesis first, left to right*

    3 * **2** * (8 + 4)   *parenthesis first*

    3 * 2 * **12**   *if same level(*, /), work from left to right*

       6 * 12

          72

E. -3 * (6 * (3 - 8) + 10)   *inner-most parenthesis first*

    -3 * (6 * **-5** + 10)   *if same level (+ and -), work from left to right*

    -3 * (**-30** + 10)   *parenthesis first*

    -3 * **-20**   *the minus in front of 3: -3, is a sign, not an operator*

       60

Variables and Functions

If there are variables and functions in an expression, replace the variables with their current values (shown below); evaluate any functions; and then evaluate using the rules for the order of operation given above:

Examples:

X	Y	Z
4	5	6

A.   Z - X mod Y   *replace variables with current values*

   6 - 4 mod 5   *mod takes precedence over - , 4/5=0 with 4 remainder!*

   6 - 4   *4 mod 5=4, the 4 replaces 4 mod 5 on this line*

    2   *6-4=2, the 2 replaces 6-4 on this line: Done!*

B.   Z - sqr(X)   *replace variables with current values*

   6 - sqr (4)   *The square root of 4 is 2*

   6 - 2   *The 2 replaces sqr(4) on this line*

    4   *6-2=4, the 4 replaces 6-2 on this line: Done!*

C.   z - sqr(X+Y)   *replace variables with current values*

   6 - sqr(4+5)   *Add 4+5 before evaluating the function*

   6 - sqr(9)   *The square root of 9 is 3*

   6 - 3   *The 3 replaces sqr(9) on this line*

    3   *6-3=3, the 3 replaces 6-3 on this line: Done!*

D.   (X + Y + Z) / 3   *replace variables with current values*

   (4 + 5 + 6) / 3   *parenthesis first: + from left to right*

   (9 + 6) / 3   *parenthesis first*

       15 / 3   *Notice that this is the average of the 3 numbers:*

       5   *What is the result is the parenthesis are left out?*

Exercise: Evaluate each expression, use the values of x, y and z shown below: check your answers using the debug window.

X	Y	Z
3	7	9

1. X + Y * Z

2. (X + Y) * Z

3. Z / 2 + X

4. Z / (2 + X)

5. Z mod 2 + X

6. Z mod (2 + X)

7. X * sqr(Z)

8. X * sqr(Z+Y)

Algebra

Many times a programmer is given an algebraic formula, and must write an assignment statement that will correctly calculate the answer. After writing a statement, check it by hand, using sample values and the method shown above to verify that the equation is correct. Use the following guidelines to convert algebraic expressions to programming statements:

Algebra	Program	Explanation:
XY	X*Y	Algebra uses single letters for variables, and can omit the *, programming languages always require an operator.
$X \cdot Y$	X*Y	Algebra sometimes uses a dot for multiplication.
X^2	X^2	Programming languages use only one line for equations: they can not write anything above or below the line.
X^Z	X^Z	The ^ operator is used for any power
$\sqrt{X}$	sqr(X)	The sqr function returns the square root
$\dfrac{A+B}{C}$	(A+B)/C	Compound numerators and divisors must be enclosed in parenthesis: Notice the difference between this example and the one below:
$A+\dfrac{B}{C}$	A+B/C	Notice the difference between this example and the one above.

Remember: Algebra uses single letters for variables: programmers should use good variable names wherever possible!

The "Grade" program calculates the average of the midterm and final with the equation:
```
Average = (Midterm + Final) / 2
```

Assume that the midterm grade is 80 and the final grade is 90. Average will be calculated as shown below:

$$(\underline{80 + 90}) \ / \ 2 \qquad \qquad \textit{parenthesis first}$$
$$\underline{\quad 170 \quad} \ / \ 2$$
$$85$$

What will the average be if you leave off the parenthesis?

The "Grade" Program

Start a new project (select <u>F</u>ile, <u>N</u>ew Project)

① Build the form shown below:

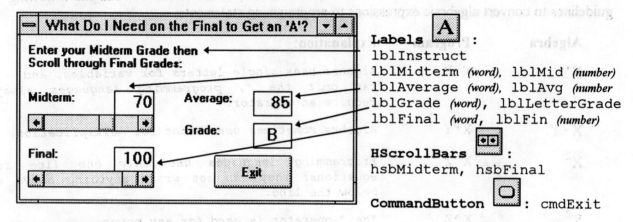

Labels [A] :
lblInstruct
lblMidterm *(word)*, lblMid *(number)*
lblAverage *(word)*, lblAvg *(number*
lblGrade *(word)*, lblLetterGrade
lblFinal *(word*, lblFin *(number)*

HScrollBars [◄►] :
hsbMidterm, hsbFinal

CommandButton [O] : cmdExit

② Change the properties (including the names):

```
Form frmGrade
    Caption    =    " What Do I Need on the Final to Get an 'A'?"
Label lblInstruct
    Caption    =    "Enter your Midterm Grade then ✪
                     ✪ Scroll through Final Grades:"
Label lblGrade
    Alignment     =    2   'Center
    BorderStyle   =    1   'Fixed Single
    Caption       =    "F"
Label lblLetterGrade
    Caption       =    "Grade:"
Label lblAvg
    Alignment     =    1   'Right Justify
    BorderStyle   =    1   'Fixed Single
    Caption       =    "0"
Label lblAverage
    Caption       =    "Average:"
Label lblFinal
    Caption       =    "Final:"
Labels lblFin, lblMid
    Alignment     =    1   'Right Justify
    BorderStyle   =    1   'Fixed Single
    Caption       =    "0"
Label lblMidterm
    Caption       =    "Midterm:"
HScrollBars hsbMidterm, hsbFinal
    Min       =    0
    Max       =    100
CommandButton cmdExit
    Caption = "E&xit"
```

③ Write the code for the "Grade" Program:

```
Sub cmdExit_Click ()
  End
End Sub

Sub computeGrade () ' A general procedure
Dim avg
    avg = (hsbMidterm + hsbFinal) / 2
    lblAvg = avg
    'caption is default property, lblAvg is same as lblAvg.caption
    If avg >= 90 Then
       lblGrade = "A"
    ElseIf avg >= 80 Then
       lblGrade = "B"
    ElseIf avg >= 70 Then
       lblGrade = "C"
    ElseIf avg >= 65 Then
       lblGrade = "D"
    Else lblGrade = "F"
    End If
End Sub

Sub hsbFinal_Change ()
  lblFin.Caption = hsbFinal.Value
  computeGrade
End Sub

Sub hsbFinal_Scroll ()
  hsbFinal_Change     'call the change procedure
End Sub

Sub hsbMidterm_change ()
  lblMid.Caption = hsbMidterm.Value
  computeGrade
End Sub

Sub hsbMidterm_Scroll ()
  hsbMidterm_change   'call the change procedure
End Sub
```

④ Save the file as `B:\grade.frm`, save the project as `B:\grade.mak`

The procedure `ComputeGrade( )` could also be written using the `Select Case` statement:

```
Sub computeGrade ()
Dim avg
    avg = (hsbMidterm + hsbFinal) / 2
    lblAvg = avg
    Select Case avg
      Case 0 To 64: lblGrade = "F"
      Case 65 To 69: lblGrade = "D"
      Case 70 To 79: lblGrade = "C"
      Case 80 To 89: lblGrade = "B"
      Case 90 To 100: lblGrade = "A"
    End Select
End Sub
```

The "Inches to Centimeters" Program

The "Inches to Centimeters" program uses a scroll bar to select inches, the value is displayed both as total inches, feet and inches and centimeters.

① **Start a new project** (select **File, New Project**) **and build the form shown below:**

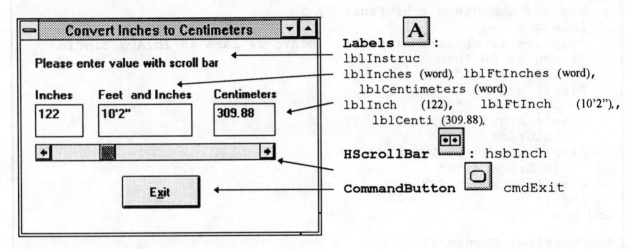

Labels ⬛ :
lblInstruc
lblInches (word), lblFtInches (word),
    lblCentimeters (word)
lblInch (122), lblFtInch (10'2"),,
    lblCenti (309.88),

HScrollBar : hsbInch

CommandButton cmdExit

② **Change the properties** (including the names):

```
Form frmInch
    Caption             =     "Convert Inches to Centimeters"
Label lblInstruc
    Caption             =     "Please enter value with scroll bar"
Labels lblInch, lblFtInch, lblCenti
    BorderStyle         =     1  'Fixed Single
    Caption             =     " "
Label lblInches
    Caption             =     "Inches"
Label lblFtInches
    Caption             =     "Feet  and Inches"
Label lblCentimeters
    Caption             =     "Centimeters"
HScrollBar hsbInch
    Max                 =     500
CommandButton cmdExit
    Caption             =     "E&xit"
```

③ **Write the code for the "Inches" Program:**

```
Sub cmdExit_Click ()
 End
End Sub

Sub hsbInch_Change ()
    lblInch = hsbInch.Value
    lblCenti = hsbInch.Value * 2.54
    lblFtInch = Int(hsbInch.Value / 12) & "'"  'int returns an integer
    lblFtInch = lblFtInch & hsbInch.Value Mod 12 & Chr(34) 'Prints "
End Sub
```

```
Sub hsbInch_Scroll ()
  hsbInch_Change    'call change procedure
End Sub
```

④ **Save the file** as B:\inches.frm, save the project as B:\inches.mak

Note : There is only one scroll bar: the scroll bar selects inches and the inches is converted to feet and inches and centimeters. All values are equivalent measures of different units. A common mistake is to try to use one scroll bar to select inches and another scroll bar to select centimeters: it does NOT work!

To print the double quote, as in 3'6", we must use **chr(34)** to print the ANSI value 34. We can not use **"** because double quotes are used to enclose strings in Visual Basic.

Experiment: Write a program to convert Fahrenheit to centigrade, or pounds to kilograms, or dollars to yens. The method is the same for all conversions.

Writing a Function

In addition to the built-in functions, you can write your own functions. Writing a function is similar to writing a general procedure. To illustrate functions, we will modify the grade program to use two functions. The first function, **average**, will receive two numbers and return the average. The second function, **grade**, will receive the average and return the letter grade.

The "Grade 2" Program

This program has the same result as the previous version, but uses a function to compute the average, and another function to compute the letter grade.

① **Load the grade.mak project**. Save the file as B:\grade2.frm, save the project as B:\grade2.mak

② From a Code window, select from the menu bar **View, New Procedure**
(You must be in a code window to create a function. If you are on the form, you can double-click to open a code window.)

The New Procedure dialog window opens. Select **Function**. Type the name of the function, then select OK. (OK is disabled until you type a name.) Name the function **average.**

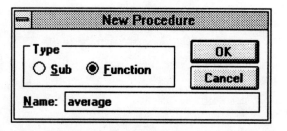

③ Insert the arguments inside the parenthesis, then write the code. The last statement that a function executes is to return a value. A value is returned by assigning the value to the name of the function. In the example, the name of the function is average: the last statement assigns a value to average.

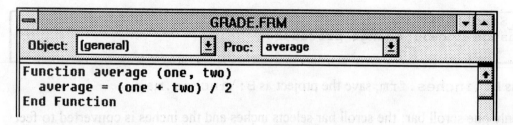

```
┌─────────────────────────────────────────────────────────┐
│ ─                        GRADE.FRM                   ▼ ▲ │
├─────────────────────────────────────────────────────────┤
│ Object: [general]        ±  Proc: average           ±    │
├─────────────────────────────────────────────────────────┤
│ Function average (one, two)                           ▲  │
│   average = (one + two) / 2                              │
│ End Function                                             │
└─────────────────────────────────────────────────────────┘
```

④ Create a second function named grade that receives the average and returns the letter grade:

```
Function grade (avg)
   If avg >= 90 Then
     grade = "A"
   ElseIf avg >= 80 Then
     grade = "B"
   ElseIf avg >= 70 Then
     grade = "C"
   ElseIf avg >= 65 Then
     grade = "D"
   Else
     grade = "F"
   End If
End Function
```

⑤ **Rewrite** the code for **computeGrade** to call the functions **average** and **grade**:

```
Sub computeGrade ()
 lblAvg = average(hsbMidterm, hsbFinal)
 lblGrade = grade(lblAvg)
End Sub
```

⑥ There are no other changes, run the program, then compare this version to the earlier version. **Save the file** as B:\grade2.frm, save the project as B:\grade2.mak

Experiment: Rewrite the "Inches to Centimeters" program to use a function.

Chapter 6

Loops

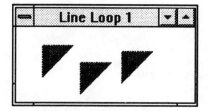

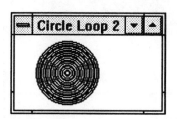

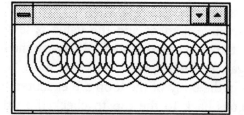

**Use FOR, WHILE
&
DO UNTIL Loops**

Nested Loops

Endless Loops

DoEvents

**Use Loops to Find
Julian Date**

Loops

A loop is a group of statements that is repeated. Visual Basic has three types of loops: **For** loops; **While** loops and **Do Until** loops.

For Loops

A **FOR** loop allows you to specify a starting value for a variable, an end value and the amount you want to change, or increment. The first format does not specify an increment: it will increment by +1:

> **For** *<variable>* = *<start value>* **to** *<end value>*
>> *<statements>*
> **Next** *<variable>*

The examples below can be entered into a new project with no controls, no property changes: The print command prints directly on the form:

```
Sub Form_Click ()
Dim x
   For x = 1 To 5
     Print x
   Next x
End Sub
```
```
1
2
3
4
5
```

The second format specifies an increment:

> **For** *<variable>* = *<start value>* **to** *<end value>* **Step** *<increment>*
>> *<statements>*
> **Next** *<variable>*

```
Sub Form_Click ()
Dim x
   For x = 2 To 10 Step 2
     Print x
   Next x
End Sub
```
```
2
4
6
8
10
```

When the For loop is executed the variable is assigned the starting value. Then the value is compared to the end value. If the increment is a positive number and the value is less than or equal to the end value, the statements in the body of the loop are executed, otherwise the next line after the loop is executed. If the increment is a negative number, then the value must be greater than or equal to the end value. After the statements in the body of the loop are executed, the next statement adds the increment to the variable and goes back to the top to check the value. The statements in a For loop may execute 0 or more times. If the starting value is past the end value it does not execute at all:

The example on the right does not print anything because x has a starting value that is greater than 1 and the increment is +1.
(If you don't specify step size, the default is +1):

```
Sub Form_Click ()
Dim x
   For x = 10 To 1
     Print x
   Next x
End Sub
```

You must specify a negative step size if the starting value is greater than the end value: This program prints 10, 9, 8, 7, 6, 5, 4, 3, 2, 1:

```
Sub Form_Click ()
Dim x
    For x = 10 To 1 Step -1
       Print x
    Next x
End Sub
```

For Loop Programs

These programs use the Circle and Line commands, no controls are placed on the form and no properties are changed except the caption of the form. Start a new project or delete the code in Form_click from the previous exercise. Run each version: click the mouse in several places, then make revisions for the next version. Save these programs as `B:\loop1.frm, loop2`, etc.

The "Circle 1" Program draws circles with a radius from 1 to 100 each time the mouse is pressed. (The click procedure does not have X and Y as arguments, so the mouseDown procedure is used.)

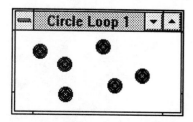

```
Sub Form_MouseDown (Button As Integer, Shift As Integer, ⇨
    ⇨ x As Single, y As Single)
Dim r
  For r = 1 To 100     'Draw circle with radius r
    Circle (x, y), r
  Next r
End Sub
```

The "Circle 2" Program draws circles with a radius from 1 to 500 with a step size of 25 each time the mouse is pressed.

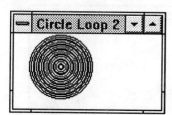

```
Sub Form_MouseDown (Button As Integer, Shift As Integer, ⇨
    ⇨ x As Single, y As Single)
Dim r
  For r = 1 To 500 Step 25
    'Draw circle with radius r
    Circle (x, y), r
  Next r
End Sub
```

The "Line Loop 1" Program draws lines with a length from 1 to 500 with a step size of 25 each time the mouse is pressed.

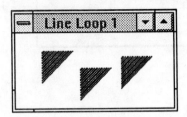

```
Sub Form_MouseDown (Button As Integer, Shift As Integer, ⇨
  ⇨ x As Single, y As Single)
Dim n
  For n = 1 To 500 Step 25
    Line (x + n, y)-(x, y + n)
  Next n
End Sub
```

The "Circle Loop 3" Program draws circles with a radius of 50. The center of each circle is a distance of 100 from the last circle.

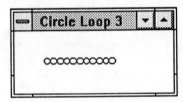

```
Sub Form_MouseDown (Button As Integer, Shift As Integer, ⇨
  ⇨ x As Single, y As Single)
Dim n
  For n = x To x + 1000 Step 100
    Circle (n, y), 50
  Next n
End Sub
```

Experiment: Try to figure out what the code below will do before you try it, then run it to see if you were right:

```
Sub Form_MouseDown (Button As Integer, Shift As Integer, ⇨
  ⇨ x As Single, y As Single)
Dim n
  For n = 0 To 1000 Step 150
    Circle (x + n, y + n), 100
  Next n
End Sub
```

DoEvents

Some loops can go on for quite a while. All other commands are ignored while the loop is executing. You can not press pause or stop, you wait!

The **DoEvents** command tells the program to take a break and see if any other event has occurred and do those events (if any). Try changing the size of the form without the DoEvents statement, then try it with the DoEvents statement:

```
Sub Form_MouseDown(Button As Integer, ⇨
 ⇨ Shift As Integer, x As Single, ⇨
 ⇨ y As Single)
Dim r
For r = 1 To 5000
 Circle (x, y), r
 'allow other events to execute
 DoEvents
Next r
End Sub
```

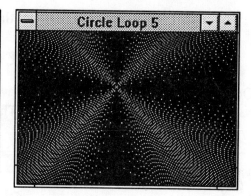

While Loops

The while loop uses a Boolean expression to determine when to end the loop:
The format of a while loop is:

> **While** <Boolean expression>
> > <*statements*>
> **Wend**

The example below can be entered into a new project with no controls, no property changes:

```
Sub Form_Click ()
Dim x
 x = 10
 While x > 0
    Print x
    x = x - 1
 Wend
 Print "Blast Off"
End Sub
```

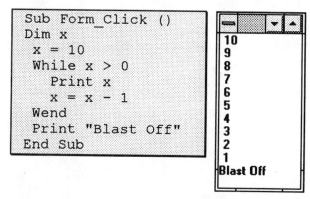

When the while loop is executed, the Boolean expression is tested: if it is true the body of the loop is executed. When it gets to the Wend statement it goes back to the top and tests again. The loop is repeated until the test fails, then the next statement after the Wend is executed. A While loop can execute zero or more times.

Note: If the Boolean expression is true, all of the statements in the loop execute, even if the expression becomes false during the loop.

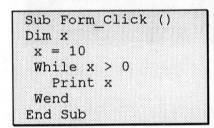

Notice that the 10 does not print but the 0 does.

Endless Loops

Occasionally, you create a loop that will never end. In the example below, the statement to subtract 1 from X has been left out. This program will print 10 over and over. Eventually the system will give you an error message:

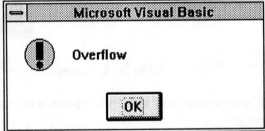

Do Loop

The Do Loop is similar to the While loop except that it does the test at the end of the loop. A do loop executes one or more times. The format of a Do Until loop is:

Do
     <statements>
Loop Until <Boolean expression>

Example:

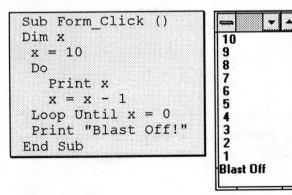

Nested Loops

A *nested* loop is a loop inside a loop. The loops do not have to be the same type. There can be a for loop inside a while loop; a for loop inside a for loop, etc. The inner loop is executed in its entirety for each execution of the outer loop.

Nested Loop Programs

The 'Circle Loop 4' program uses nested **For** loops. For each value of **n** (the outer loop), the value of **r** (the inner loop) has the values 25, 50, 75 and 100. *(Delete any code in form_click)*

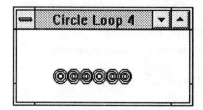

```
Sub Form_MouseDown (Button As Integer, Shift As Integer, ⇨
   ⇨ x As Single, y As Single)
Dim n, r
   For n = x To x + 1000 Step 200
      For r = 25 To 100 Step 25
        Circle (n, y), r
      Next r
   Next n
End Sub
```

The next program uses a **For** loop inside a **While** loop. For each value of **x** (the outer loop), the value of **r** (the inner loop) has the values 1, 101, 201, 301, 401 (the value of **r** starts at 1 and adds 100 at the end of the loop. When the value becomes 501 the loop ends without using the last value, 501):

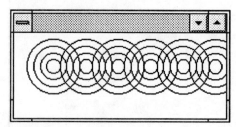

```
Sub Form_MouseDown (Button As Integer,Shift As Integer,x As Single, ⇨
   ⇨ y As Single)
 Dim r
   While x < scalewidth 'width of the form
      For r = 1 To 500 Step 100
        Circle (x, y), r
      Next r
      x = x + 500
      'the value of an argument can change!
   Wend
End Sub
```

The "Month" Program

The "Month" Program uses a *variable array*, **days**, to store the number of days in each month. The array is declared in general procedures (global). It is given values (initialized) in Form_Load. When a month is selected, the maximum of the scroll bar is set to the number of days in the month using the index of the month selected as the index to the array **days**.

① **Start a new project and build the form as shown**. *(Be sure to put the option buttons inside the frame.)*

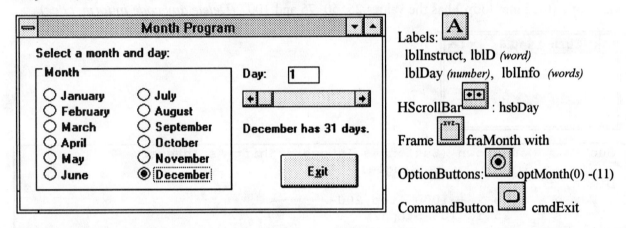

② **Change the properties, including the names**. Change the captions to match the illustration:
   HScrollBar **hsbDay**: min = 1,   max = 31, value = 1
   Label lblDay: BorderStyle = 1 - fixed single

③ **Write the code:**

```
Option Explicit
  Dim days(12)   'array of 12 numbered days(0) to days(11)

Sub cmdExit_Click ()'end the program
  End
End Sub

Sub Form_Load ()  'Initialize the array
  days(0) = 31 'January
  days(1) = 28 'February
  days(2) = 31 'March
  days(3) = 30 'April
  days(4) = 31 'May
  days(5) = 30 'June
  days(6) = 31 'July
  days(7) = 31 'August
  days(8) = 30 'September
  days(9) = 31 'October
  days(10) = 30 'November
  days(11) = 31 'December
  optMonth_click (0)   'Call as if January had been selected
End Sub
```

```
Sub hsbDay_Change ()    'Copy the value of the scroll bar to lblDay
  lblDay.Caption = hsbDay.Value
End Sub

Sub hsbDay_Scroll ()    'Call hsbDay_Change to change caption
  lblDay.Caption = hsbDay.Value
End Sub

Sub optMonth_click(index As Integer)'Use index for # of days in month
  hsbDay.Max = days(index) 'Set max days for month selected
  lblInfo = optMonth(index).Caption 'May
  lblInfo = lblInfo & " has "        'May has
  lblInfo = lblInfo & days(index)    'May has 31
  lblInfo = lblInfo & " days."       'May has 31 days.
End Sub
```

④ **Save the file** as B:\month.frm, save the project as B:\month.mak

The "Julian Date" Program

The "Julian Date" Program is an enhancement to the Month Program: it uses a **For** loop and a general procedure to calculate the Julian date. The Julian date is the day of the year: January 1 is day 1; February 1 is day 32, etc. To find the Julian date of May 21st, add the number of days in January, February, March and April, then add 21 to the total. A total is found by setting total to zero, then adding numbers to it: total = total + num.

① **Load the month.mak project.**

Save the file as B:\julian.frm, save the project as B:\julian.mak

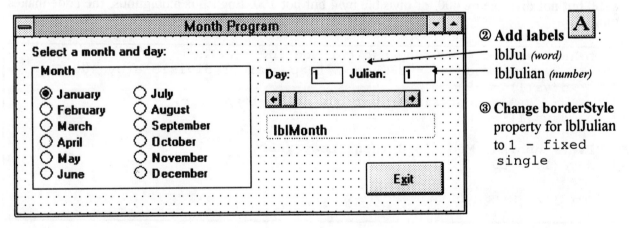

② **Add labels** [A]:
—— lblJul *(word)*
—— lblJulian *(number)*

③ **Change borderStyle** property for lblJulian to 1 - fixed single

④ **Add to the existing code:**

```
Option Explicit
  Dim days(12)    'array of 12: numbered 0..11
  Dim mthIndex    'set when month changes, instead of big IF to see which month
```

```
Sub hsbDay_Change () 'call Julian whenever the day changes
  lblDay.Caption = hsbDay.Value
  Julian
End Sub

Sub optMonth_click(index As Integer)'Use index for # of days in month
 hsbDay.Max = days(index) 'Set max days for month selected
 lblInfo = optMonth(index).Caption 'May
 lblInfo = lblInfo & " has "        'May has
 lblInfo = lblInfo & days(index)    'May has 31
 lblInfo = lblInfo & " days."       'May has 31 days.
 mthIndex = index       'so Julian will know what month it is
 Julian                 'call Julian when month changes
End Sub

Sub Julian () 'A general procedure: all of this is new
  Dim mth      'local variables
  Dim total
  total = 0
  For mth = 0 To mthIndex - 1   'for all the months prior,
    total = total + days(mth)   'add # of days in that month
  Next mth
  total = total + hsbDay.Value 'add day of month
  lblJulian.caption = total      'display the Julian date
End Sub
```

Note: These two programs use 28 for the number of days in February. You can solve the leap year problem by printing a message "Add 1 if leap year" if the month is any month after February. You can also add a scroll bar hsbYear to select year. A year is a leap year if it is divisible by 4 and 100 but not divisible by 400, or divisible by 4 but not 100. English is ambiguous, the code makes it clear:

```
If hsbYear Mod 4 = 0 And hsbYear Mod 100 = 0 Then
  If hsbYear Mod 400 = 0 Then   'Leap year if divisible by 400
    days(1) = 29
  Else     ' a centesimal year but not a leap year.
    days(1) = 28
  End If
ElseIf hsbYear Mod 4 = 0 Then 'Leap year
 days(1) = 29
Else
 days(1) = 28
End If
```

Chapter 7

Move It!

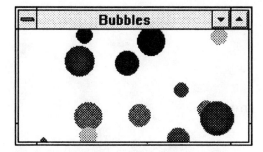

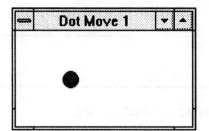

Use a Timer

Learn About Random Numbers

Use Loops & Timers for Animation

Write a Function & A Module

The Timer

The controls that we have used so far had procedures that were executed in response to mouse events: clicking, double-clicking, or moving. The timer control has just one procedure, *timer* that is executed at regular intervals. The interval is a property that can be changed: smaller values for interval mean that the timer "goes off" faster. Large values for interval mean that the action is slower. If the interval is set to 0 (the default value), the timer is "deactivated".

The Counter Program

The Counter Program increments (adds 1 to) a counter when the timer "goes off."

① **Build the form:**

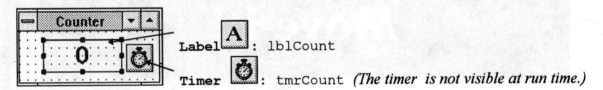

Label [A] : lblCount

Timer [⏱] : tmrCount *(The timer is not visible at run time.)*

② **Change the properties** (including the names)

```
Form frmCounter
    Caption             =      "Counter"
Timer tmrCount
    Interval            =      1
Label lblCount
    Alignment           =      2    'Center
    BorderStyle         =      1    'Fixed Single
    Caption             =      "0"
    FontSize            =      18
```

③ **Write the Code for the Counter Program:**

```
Sub tmrCount_Timer ()
   lblCount = lblCount + 1
End Sub
```

④ **Save the file** as B:\counter.frm, save the project as B:\counter.mak

Experiment: Reset the counter when you click the mouse. Change the interval of the timer.

Variation: When you run this variation, the background color cycles through the 16 QBColors.

Delete the label. Change the interval on the timer to 1000. Change the code:

```
Option Explicit
Dim color  'declare global variable

Sub Form_Load ()
 color = 0  'initialize color to 0
End Sub
```

```
Sub tmrCount_Timer ()
 color = color + 1  'Increment color
 If color > 15 Then color = 0  'Reset color to 0
 caption = "Color " & color 'Show color in the caption (of the form)
 backcolor = QBColor(color) 'Change background color (of the form)
End Sub
```

Random Numbers

The function RND generates a random number from 0 to 1. However, most of the time, you will need a random integer within a certain range: for example a random number from 1 to 6 for rolling dice, or a random number from 0 to scalewidth to pick a random column on the screen. To use RND to generate a random integer within a range use the format:

$$<variable> = \textbf{INT (RND} * <range>) + <minimum>$$

Example: Die is to be a random numbers from 1 to 6. There are 6 numbers in the range, minimum is 1: **Die = INT(RND*6)+1**

Example: N is to be a random integer from 50 to 60. There are 11 numbers in the range, minimum is 50: **N = INT(RND*11)+50**

The Bubbles Program

The Bubbles Program illustrates random numbers using the circle method.

① Start a new project, save the form and project as B:\BUBBLE.FRM and B:\BUBBLE.MAK

② There is nothing on the form except a timer: change the properties as follows:

```
Form frmBubble
   Caption    = "Bubbles"
   FillStyle  = 0  'Solid
   ScaleMode  = 3  'Pixel

Timer   Timer1
   Interval  = 10
```

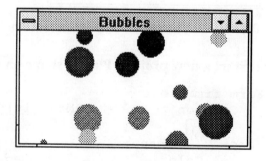

The bubbles appear at run time, the timer does not.

③ Add the code:

```
Sub Timer1_Timer ()'draw circles a random color, radius, X and Y
   Dim X, Y, radius, color    ' Declare variables
   X = Int(Rnd * ScaleWidth)  ' Set X position, anywhere on screen.
   Y = Int(Rnd * ScaleHeight) ' Set Y position, anywhere on screen
   color = Int(Rnd * 16)      ' color is random 0..15
   fillColor = QBColor(color)
   radius = Int(Rnd * 15) + 3 ' radius is 3..17
   Circle (X, Y), radius, QBColor(color) 'Draw the circle
End Sub
```

Note: If you run the program above a few times, you will notice that it always draws the same dots. If you want the picture to be different each time, the random number seed must be set using randomize:

```
Sub Form_Load()
    Randomize
End Sub
```

④ **Save the file.**

Programmers sometimes wait and add the randomize command after the program is debugged. If a mistake occurs during execution, you can change the code, then run the program again to see if the error is corrected. If you include the randomize command at the beginning, it is very hard to get the same sequence of numbers to occur again to see if the error has been corrected.

Experiment: write a program to draw random lines.

Movement

The position of a shape or other object can be changed by changing the value of **left** or **top.** The diagram below shows the properties that you will use to change the position of a shape:

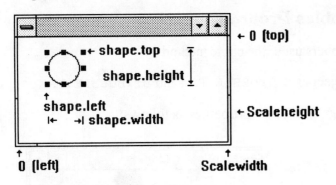

Note: the shape does not have properties right and bottom.

The right edge of the shape is
`shape.left+shape.width`

The bottom edge of the shape is
`shape.top+shape.height`

① **Start a new project: Place a shape on the form and change the name and properties:**

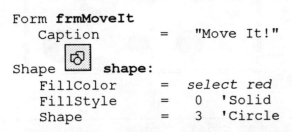

```
Form frmMoveIt
    Caption        =    "Move It!"

Shape  [icon]  shape:
    FillColor      =    select red
    FillStyle      =    0   'Solid
    Shape          =    3   'Circle
```

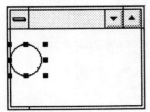

Drag the sides of the shape so that the circle fits perfectly, (shown on left). If the rectangle is too big, the statements below will move the rectangle to the edge, but it won't look like the circle is on the edge (shown on right).

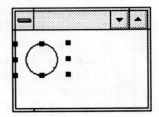

② **Run the program**, then press pause 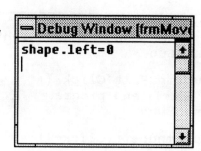 so that you can try the statements below in the DEBUG Window.

The statements below will move the shape to an edge:

```
shape.left = 0  ' Move the shape to the left edge of the form
shape.top = 0   ' Move the shape to the top of the form
shape.top = ScaleHeight-shape.height   ' Move the shape to the bottom of the form
shape.left = ScaleWidth-shape.width ' Move the shape to the right edge of the form
```

(The statement `shape.top=ScaleHeight` *will move the shape below the form: the top edge of the shape on the bottom edge of the form)*

The statements below will move the shape one position from its current position. the movement is very small, try 10 if you prefer. You can repeat a statement in the debug window by moving the cursor to the line and pressing ⏎Enter.

```
shape.left = shape.left-1   ' move the shape one position to the left
shape.left = shape.left+1   ' move the shape one position to the right
shape.top = shape.top-1     ' move the shape up one position
shape.top = shape.top+1     ' move the shape  down one position
```

Note: The size of 1 position depends on the `ScaleMode` property of the form. Add the code below, then run the program. Try different values of ScaleMode: inch, pixel, etc.

```
Sub Form_Click ()
  shape.Left = shape.Left + 1
End Sub
```

The Corners Program

The Corners Program uses a menu to move the shape to the corners.

③ **Add a Menu** 🗒 **to the MoveIt program according to the table below:**

Caption	Name
E&xit	mnuExit
&Top	mnuTop
&Bottom	mnuBottom
&Left	mnuLeft
&Right	mnuRight

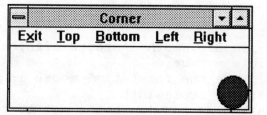

④ **Delete the code in Form_Click and add the code shown on the next page:**
Try to write the code on your own without looking!

```
Sub mnuBottom_Click ()
  shape.Top = scaleHeight - shape.Height
End Sub

Sub mnuExit_Click ()
  End  'end program
End Sub

Sub mnuLeft_Click ()
  shape.Left = 0
End Sub

Sub mnuRight_Click ()
  shape.Left = scalewidth - shape.Width
End Sub

Sub mnuTop_Click ()
  shape.Top = 0
End Sub
```

⑤ **Save the file** as B:\corners.frm, save the project as B:\corners.mak

The Moving Dot Program

The Moving Dot Program uses a **For** loop to move a dot. The dot is not visible until the mouse is clicked. When the mouse is clicked, the dot moves in on the left, travels across the form and disappears off the right side.

① **Start a new project. Build the form:**

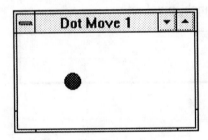

Form frmMove: Caption = "Dot Move 1"

Shape : shpDot

```
FillColor   =    select a color you like
FillStyle   =    0    'Solid
Shape       =    3    'Circle
Visible     =    false
```
fit the shape to the circle as before.

② **Write the code:**

```
Sub Form_Click ()              'move dot from left to right
Dim x, start
  start = 0 - shpDot.Width  'starts off the form on left
  shpDot.visible = true
  'becomes visible the first time mouse is clicked
  For x = start To scalewidth
    shpDot.Left = x       'move the dot to the right
  Next x
End Sub
```

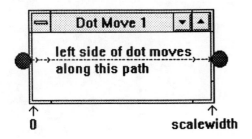

Explanation: the left side of the form is column 0, the right side is the scalewidth of the form.

The dot starts at 0 minus the width of the dot. It becomes visible as it moves onto the form. When it gets to the right, it keeps moving off the form until the left side is at scalewidth.

③ **Save the file** as B:\dotmove1.frm, save the project as B:\dotmove1.mak

The Timer

The next program does exactly the same thing as the one above, but moves the dot when the timer "goes off" instead of when the mouse is clicked.

① **Add a timer** ⏱ to the form: **timer1**

② **Change the interval property of the timer to 1000.**

③ **Move the code from** Form_Click **to** Timer1_Timer:

Highlight the code in **Form_Click** and press Ctrl+X, find the **Timer1_Timer** procedure and press Ctrl+V to paste the code into **Timer1_Timer**.

```
Sub Timer1_Timer ()
Dim x, start
  start = 0 - shpDot.Width  'starts off the form on left
  shpDot.Visible = True  'show the dot
  For x = start To scalewidth
    shpDot.Left = x         'move the dot to the right
  Next x
  shpDot.Visible = False 'hide the dot
End Sub
```

④ **Save the file** as B:\dotmove2.frm, save the project as B:\dotmove2.mak

The Moving Dot 3 Program

The Moving Dot 3 Program moves the dot 1 position each time the timer goes off. There is no For loop. The dot changes direction when the user selects option buttons for left or right.

① **Add Option Buttons** ⦿ : optLeft, optRight

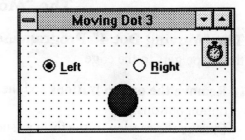

② **Change the properties (including the name)**

```
Form frmMove
   Caption          =     "Moving Dot 3"
Timer timer1
   Interval         =     1
OptionButton optRight
   Caption          =     "&Right"
OptionButton optLeft
   Caption          =     "&Left"
   Value            =     True
```

③ **Write the Code for the Moving Dot 3 Program:**

Add a variable `direction` in (general), declarations:

```
Option Explicit
Dim direction

Sub Form_Load ()
   direction = -1
End Sub

Sub optLeft_Click ()
   direction = -1
End Sub

Sub optRight_Click ()
   direction = 1
End Sub

Sub Timer1_Timer ()   'Delete the previous code
   shpDot.Left = shpDot.Left + direction * 10
End Sub
```

Experiment: Run the program, let the dot go off the edge of the form. Press Pause, go to debug: check the value of **shpDot.Left** and ScaleWidth (width of form). Change the values.

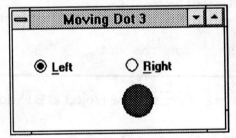

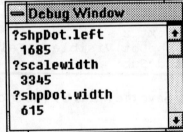

④ **Save the file** as B:\dotmove3.frm, save the project as B:\dotmove3.mak

The "Moving Dot 4" Program

The "Moving Dot 4" Program uses an IF statement to automatically change direction when the shape gets to the edge.

① **Remove the option buttons** and the code for the option buttons.
Change the caption of the form as shown.

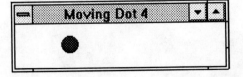

② **Add Code:**

```
Sub Timer1_Timer()
  shpDot.Left = shpDot.Left + direction *10
  If shpDot.Left < 0 Then          'Shape is at left edge
    Beep
    direction = 1
  End If
  If shpDot.Left + shpDot.Width > ScaleWidth Then
    Beep                      'Shape is at right edge
    direction = -1
  End If
End Sub
```

④ **Save the file** as B:\dotmove4.frm, save the project as B:\dotmove4.mak

The Moving Dot 5 Program

This program uses a scroll bar for the amount the shape moves instead of +10 and -10.

① **Add to the form:**

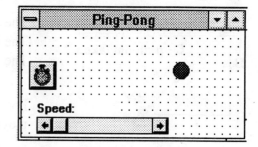

HScrollBar : **hsbSpeed**
    min =0, max =50

Label : **lblSpeed**
    caption = "Speed:"

② **Set the ScaleMode property of the form to 3 - Pixel**.

③ **Modify the code for the timer:**

```
Sub Timer1_Timer ()
  shpOne.Left = shpOne.Left + direction * hsbSpeed
  'Uses value on hsbSpeed instead of the constant 1
  If shpDot.Left < 0 Then
    Beep
    direction = 1
  End If
  If shpDot.Left + shpDot.Width > frmMove.ScaleWidth Then
    Beep
    direction = -1
  End If
End Sub
```

④ **Save the file** as B:\dotmove5.frm, save the project as B:\dotmove5.mak

Experiment: Change the ScaleMode property for the form and run the program for each value. Change the size of the form during execution. Add code to display the speed.

Run the Program: Programmers learn to program by programming! Experiment! Try any of the ideas below; think up ideas of your own, the weirder the better!

- Try increasing the speed every time it changes direction;

- Let the shape move around the edge of the form;

- Have the shape get bigger going one direction; smaller in the other direction.

- Include a second timer with a larger interval. Change direction whenever the second timer goes off.

The "Come Here Dot" Program

The "Come Here Dot" Program moves the dot to the position the mouse is clicked in a straight line. The program uses a function to calculate the hypotenuse of a right triangle. The Form is the same as before.

The Logic:

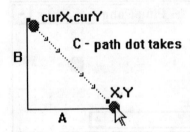

The distance from **curX** to **X** is side **A** of a right triangle. The distance from **curY** to **Y** is side **B**.

The hypotenuse, side **C** is found with the formula $c = \sqrt{a^2 + b^2}$

For each unit of C, **top** must move A/C units. **Left** must move B/C units.

When the mouse is pressed *(the mouse_down procedure is used because mouse_click doesn't have X and Y as arguments),* the starting point is found:

```
curX = shpDot.Left
curY = shpDot.Top
```

The arguments X and Y give the location where the mouse is clicked: notice in the illustration that the mouse is in the middle of the dot (the original X and Y values), but the destination is above and to the left by half the width and height of the shape:

```
x = x - shpDot.Width / 2    'destination of top left corner..
y = y - shpDot.Height / 2   '.. so middle of shape is at mouse
```

Next, the length of side A and side B are found. These values may be negative, but that is OK because, those values are the amount we want to move the shape. The length of side C (the hypotenuse of a right triangle) is found by passing A and B to the function hypo.

```
a = x - curX  'Find length of side A
b = y - curY  'Find length of side A
c = hypo(a, b)'call function hypo to find length of side C
```

A For loop generates each point along the hypotenuse. The new location is found by calculating the new point in relation to the origin. (*Incrementing*: `shpDot.Top=shDot.Top+b/c` *does not work as well because B/C is probably a fraction.*)

① **Open** `dotmove1.mak.` Change the visible property of the shape to true.
Delete the code in `form_click` and add the code below:

```
Sub Form_MouseDown (Button As Integer, Shift As Integer, ⟳
   ⟳ x As Single, y As Single)
   'Move shpDot from its current location to X,Y
   Dim curX, curY, a, b, c, cStep
   curX = shpDot.Left          'starting point
   curY = shpDot.Top
   x = x - shpDot.Width / 2  'destination of top left corner..
   y = y - shpDot.Height / 2 '.. so middle of shape is at mouse
   a = x - curX                'Find length of side A
   b = y - curY                'Find length of side A
   c = hypo(a, b)              'call function hypo to find side C
   For cStep = 0 To c          'move along hypotenuse
     shpDot.Left = curX + cStep * a / c
     shpDot.Top = curY + cStep * b / c
   Next cStep
End Sub

Function hypo (a, b) 'Create a general function to find hypotenuse
   hypo = Int(Sqr(a ^ 2 + b ^ 2))
End Function
```

② **Save the file** as B:\dotcome.frm, save the project as B:\dotcome.mak

The "Moon Turns"

The moon program uses icons of the moon to create an animated program with the moon turning. (These icons come with Visual Basic.)

① **Start a new project. Build the form as shown:**

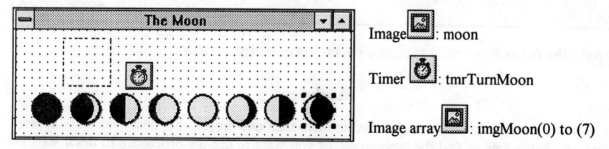

Image ⬚ : moon

Timer ⏱ : tmrTurnMoon

Image array ⬚ : imgMoon(0) to (7)

② **Change the properties, including the names and the picture for each imgMoon.**

```
Form frmMoon
   Caption      = "The Moon"
   BackColor    = ... select deep blue
Timer tmrMoon
   Interval     = 500
```

```
Image moon
   Stretch        = -1 'True
   Visible        = -1 'True
Image imgMoon(0) t0 imgMoon(7)
   Index          = 0 to 7
   Picture        = C:\VB\ICONS\ELEMENTS\MOON01.ICO to MOON08.ICO
   Visible        = 0  'False
```

Note: The images of the moon, **imgMoon(0) to imgMoon(7),** are not visible at run time. The image **Moon** is visible, the pictures in imgMoon(view) are copied into the image Moon at each timer interval. View cycles from 0 to 7, then back to 0. Set the timer interval to a value that works best on your computer. You can make the moon bigger by setting its **stretch** property to true and dragging the shape at design time. For added effect, some random stars are added each time the moon turns.

③ **Write the Code:**

```
Option Explicit
Dim view

Sub Form_Load ()
 Randomize
End Sub

Sub stars ()  'A general procedure draws 25 random "stars"
 Dim star, x, y
 For star = 1 To 25
    x = Int(Rnd * Scalewidth) 'any column
    y = Int(Rnd * Scaleheight)'any row
    PSet (x, y), QBColor(15)  'make stars bright white
 Next star
End Sub

Sub tmrMoon_Timer ()
   stars  'call the stars procedure to draw 25 stars
   view = view + 1
   If view > 7 Then view = 0
   moon = imgMoon(view)
End Sub
```

④ **Save the file** as B:\moon.frm, save the project as B:\moon.mak

Modules

Some functions and variables may be used in more than one project. Suppose you write several programs that use pi; or find the hypotenuse; or you want to use the procedure to draw stars in another project. A module has variables and functions that are independent of the form. We will recreate the moon program to use a module. Later, if you want to use these functions in another program you can include this file in the project.

① **Open** moon.mak and save the file as B:\moon2.frm, save the project as B:\moon2.mak

② **From the menu select** File, New Module

You can write code, including new procedures and functions, just like you wrote code for the form.

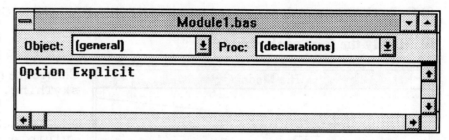

③ **Write the following code for the module:** (Pi and Hypo are included as examples, they are not used in the Moon project.) Save the module as **STARS.BAS**

```
Option Explicit
Global Const PI = 3.141592 'Pi is global to project, not the form

Function hypo (one, two)
  hypo = Sqr(one ^ 2 + two ^ 2)
End Function

Sub stars (F As Form, number As Integer)
'this is not part of a form, so we need to know which form
'to draw the stars on, number tells how many stars (instead of 25)
 Dim star, x, y
 For star = 1 To number  'number is received as argument
   x = Int(Rnd * F.ScaleWidth) 'any column on form F
   y = Int(Rnd * F.ScaleHeight)'any row on form F
   F.PSet (x, y), QBColor(15)  'draw stars on form F
 Next star
End Sub
```

③ **Save module1 as B:stars.bas**

(Select <u>W</u>indow, <u>P</u>roject. Highlight `module1.bas`, select <u>F</u>ile, `Save File As`.)

④ **Delete the procedure stars from form Moon, and modify the code:**

```
Sub tmrMoon_Timer ()
   Call stars(frmMoon, 25) 'call Global proc. Stars to draw 25 stars
   view = view + 1
   If view > 7 Then view = 0
   moon = imgMoon(view)
End Sub
```

④ **Check the project window**: This project (MOON2.MAK) should contain two files: MOON2.FRM and STARS.BAS

⑤ **Save the project.** (It has already been named.)

"Night and Day"

This project alternates between day and night: The moon moves across the form while it turns. When the moon gets to the right edge, the sun moves across the form.

① **Open the moon.mak** project and save it as NIGHT.MAK, and NIGHT.FRM

② **Modify the form as shown:**.

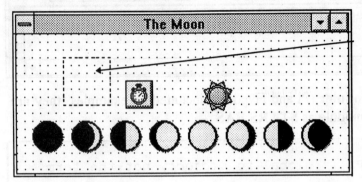

Change the name of the moon image to skyThing.

Add Image :imgSun
 visible = False
 picture =
C:\VB\ICONS\ELEMENTS\SUN.ICO

③ **Modify the Code:**

```
Option Explicit
Dim view, sky

Sub moonTurn () 'A general procedure
  Call stars(frmMoon, 1)'call Global stars procedure to draw 1 stars
  view = view + 1
  If view > 7 Then view = 0
  skyThing = imgMoon(view)
  skyThing.Left = skyThing.Left + 15
  If skyThing.Left > scalewidth Then
     caption = "The Sun"
     sky = 1   'DayTime
     skyThing = imgSun
     backColor = QBColor(14)
     skyThing.Left = -1 * skyThing.Width
  End If
End Sub

Sub sunMove ()
  skyThing.Left = skyThing.Left + 15
  If skyThing.Left > scalewidth Then
     caption = "The Moon"
     sky = 0   'NightTime
     skyThing = imgMoon(view)
     backColor = QBColor(1)
     skyThing.Left = -1 * skyThing.Width   'Off the form on left
  End If
End Sub

Sub tmrMoon_Timer () 'Delete previous code
  If sky = 0 Then moonTurn Else sunMove
End Sub
```

④ **Save the file** as B:\night.frm, save the project as B:\night.mak

Chapter 8

Talk to the User

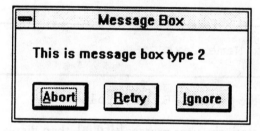

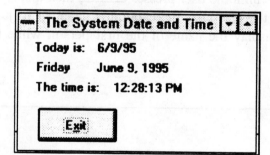

Use
Text Boxes

Input Boxes

Message
Boxes

Change the System
Date & Time

Entering Text

At this point, we have used the mouse to enter all of the information the program needed. (Scroll bars, option buttons, check boxes, command buttons, and menu choices.) There are some kinds of information that the user must type. In this chapter, we will look at ways for the user to enter text.

Text Boxes: ab

The "Hello" program uses a text box for the user to type his name. As the user types, the name appears (letter by letter) in the caption.

① Build the form as shown:

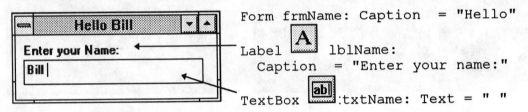

```
Form frmName: Caption = "Hello"

Label       lblName:
    Caption = "Enter your name:"

TextBox      :txtName: Text = " "
```

② Write The Code: *(notice the space in* `"Hello "`*: without the space you'll see* `"HelloBill"`

```
Sub txtName_Change ()
  frmName.Caption = "Hello " & txtName.Text
End Sub
```

③ Save the file as B:\hello1.frm, save the project as B:\hello1.mak

The next version of the Hello Program waits until the user presses ⏎Enter, then displays the name in the caption. When a change is made in the text box, the caption is changed to just "Hello". without this line, the caption would still display the name of the first person while the second person was typing his name.

④ Modify the Code: *(the form is the same)*

```
Sub txtName_Change ()
  caption = "Hello"
End Sub

Sub txtName_KeyPress (keyAscii As Integer)
  If keyAscii = 13 Then   'Ascii 13 is ENTER
    frmName.Caption = "Hello " & txtName.Text
  End If
End Sub
```

⑤ Save the file as B:\hello2.frm, save the project as B:\hello2.mak

Input Boxes

The user could overlook a text box: if you really want the users attention, use an input box. The input box pops up as shown on the right. It stays open until the user selects OK or Cancel or presses ⏎Enter.

The statement to open an input box is:

```
<var>=InputBox(<prompt>,<title>,<default>)
```

In this illustration, the prompt is "What is your name?" The title is "Name". No default is shown.

The programmer can not control the position or size of the input box.

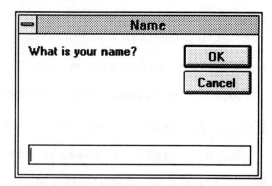

The "Hello 3" program uses the input box shown above to ask the user his name. After the user enters his name, the input box closes and the name is shown in the caption.

① **Build the form**: change the captions and names as shown:

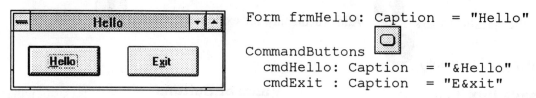

```
Form frmHello: Caption  = "Hello"

CommandButtons
    cmdHello: Caption  = "&Hello"
    cmdExit : Caption  = "E&xit"
```

② **Write the code:**

```
Sub cmdExit_Click () 'End the program
  End
End Sub

Sub cmdHello_Click () 'Ask the user his name and display in caption
Dim userName
  userName = InputBox("What is your name?", "Name")
  caption = "Hello " & userName
End Sub
```

③ **Save the file** as `B:\hello3.frm`, save the project as `B:\hello3.mak`

Message Boxes

A message box is similar to an input box. The message box can be used as either a function (returns an answer) or a statement (no answer returned) The programmer can select the type of message box to display. The type indicates which command buttons to display: Yes, No, OK, Cancel, Abort, Retry, etc.

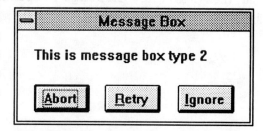

There are two formats for opening a message box:

As a function:

```
<answer> = msgBox(<Message>,<type>,<Title>)
```

As a statement:

```
msgBox <Message>,type,<Title>
```

In the illustration above, the Message is "This is message box type 2"
The title is "Message Box"

If this message box is opened as a function the statement is:

```
Answer = msgBox("This is message box type 2",2,"Message Box")
```

If you don't care what the user selects, you can open it with the statement:

```
msgBox "This is message box type 2", 2 ,"Message Box"
```

The table below shows the buttons displayed for each type, and the value returned when msgBox is used as a function. There are 6 combinations of buttons that can be displayed. You can also

display an icon along with these buttons. Add 16 to the type to display the stop icon . Add

32 to display the question mark . Add 48 display an exclamation point . Add 64 to

display the letter I (information) .

Message Box Type:

Type	Buttons Displayed
0	Ok
1	Ok, Cancel
2	Abort, Retry,Ignore
3	Yes, No, Cancel
4	Yes, No
5	Retry, Cancel

Value of Buttons

Button	Value
Ok	1
Cancel	2
Abort	3
Retry	4
Ignore	5
Yes	6
No	7

The Message Box Program

This program allows you to look at each type message box. You can select a type with the scroll bar, then press **Show Message** to open the message box. The value of the button you select will be displayed in lblAnswer.

① **Start a new project and build the form. Change the names, captions and borders as shown:**

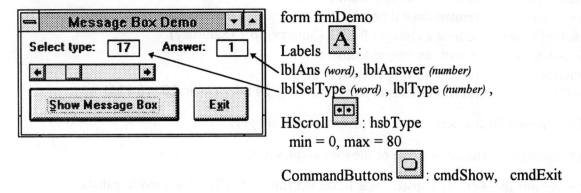

form frmDemo

Labels 🅰 :

lblAns *(word)*, lblAnswer *(number)*

lblSelType *(word)* , lblType *(number)* ,

HScroll ◄► : hsbType

min = 0, max = 80

CommandButtons ▢ : cmdShow,   cmdExit

② **Add the code:**

```
Sub cmdExit_Click ()
   End
End Sub

Sub cmdShow_Click ()
Dim msg, answer
   msg = "This is message box type " & hsbType
   lblAnswer = MsgBox(msg, hsbType, "Message Box")
End Sub

Sub hsbType_Change ()        'Copy code to Sub hsbType_Scroll ()
   lblType = hsbType
End Sub
```

③ **Run the program:** Select a type with the scroll bar, try clicking different responses.

④ **Save the file** as B:\message.frm, save the project as B:\message.mak

The System Date

Message Boxes are often used to display error message or warnings. The "System Date" Program uses a message box when the user tries to set the date to an invalid date.

The "System Date" Program (a useful application - be sure to save it!) allows the user to set the system date and time. This program is written in two parts: First we will write the program to view the date and time, then we will add commands to change the date and time. The program uses several of the built-in date and time functions.

Built-In Functions for Date and Time

Visual Basic has several built-in functions to return information about the system date and time:

Now: returns the current system date and time as a double precision number, the date is to the left of the decimal, the time is to the right of the decimal. **Now** is usually used with a function to return the specific portion you are interested in:

Day(Now)	returns an integer from 1 to 31
Month(Now)	returns an integer from 1 to 12
Year(Now)	returns the 4 digit year
Weekday(Now)	returns an integer from 1 (Sunday) to 7 (Saturday)
Second(Now)	returns an integer from 0 to 59
Minute(Now)	returns an integer from 0 to 59
Hour(Now)	returns an integer from 0 to 23 (a 24 hour clock: 20 is 8 PM)

DATE$ returns a 10 character string of the format *mm-dd-yyyy*

TIME$ returns an 8 character string of the format *hh:mm:ss*

TIMER returns the seconds elapsed since 12:00AM (midnight) Timer is used in games:

```
start=timer
...play game...
finish = Timer
playingTime = finish - start
```

Check It Out:

You can try any of these functions in the debug window without writing any code or placing controls on the form.

① Start Visual Basic

② Press the run button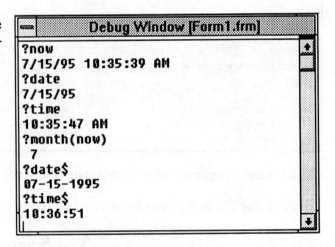

③ Press pause

(The debug window may pop up, if not, select **Window**, **Debug**.)

④ Use a question mark to print the value.

The System Date and Time Program

The System Date and Time Program - Part 1: "Look, But Don't Touch"

① **Start a new project and build the form:** Change the names, captions and borders as shown in the illustration:

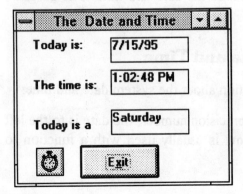

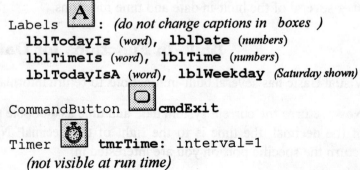

Labels **A** : *(do not change captions in boxes)*
   lblTodayIs *(word)*, **lblDate** *(numbers)*
   lblTimeIs *(word)*, **lblTime** *(numbers)*
   lblTodayIsA *(word)*, **lblWeekday** *(Saturday shown)*

CommandButton   **cmdExit**

Timer   **tmrTime:** interval=1
(not visible at run time)

② **Write the Code:**

```
Sub showDate () 'A general procedure (View, New Procedure)
Dim mthNum ' Declare variable
  mthNum = Month(Now)    'Find what month this is: an integer.
  Select Case mthNum
    Case 1: lblDate = "January"
    Case 2: lblDate = "February"
    Case 3: lblDate = "March"
    Case 4: lblDate = "April"
    Case 5: lblDate = "May"
    Case 6: lblDate = "June"
    Case 7: lblDate = "July"
    Case 8: lblDate = "August"
    Case 9: lblDate = "September"
    Case 10: lblDate = "October"
    Case 11: lblDate = "November"
    Case 12: lblDate = "December"
  End Select
 lblDate = lblDate & " " & Day(Now) & ", " & Year(Now)
End Sub

Function DayofWeek (d) 'Receives date, returns day of week
Dim dayNum
  If IsDate(d) Then
    dayNum = Weekday(d)'the built-in function returns an integer
    Select Case dayNum
      Case 1: DayofWeek = "Sunday"
      Case 2: DayofWeek = "Monday"
      Case 3: DayofWeek = "Tuesday"
      Case 4: DayofWeek = "Wednesday"
      Case 5: DayofWeek = "Thursday"
      Case 6: DayofWeek = "Friday"
      Case 7: DayofWeek = "Saturday"
    End Select
  Else DayofWeek = ""
  End If
End Function

Sub tmrTime_Timer () 'update the time
    lblTime = Time
End Sub

Sub Form_Load ()
  lblDate = Date 'Date and time are built-in function to return
  lblTime = Time 'the system date and time
  lblweekDay = dayofWeek(Now) 'dayofWeek is a general function
  showDate        'showDate is a general procedures
End Sub

Sub cmdExit_Click () 'End execution
  End
End Sub
```

Save the file as B:\date1.frm, **save the project as** B:\date2.mak

Setting the System Date and Time: Part 2

Part 1 of this program let the user *see* the system date. **Part 2** lets the user *change* the system date and time. *(Don't change the system date to find out what day of the week you were born: the next program will tell you the day of week for any valid date!)*

① **Modify the form** by adding a label with instructions:

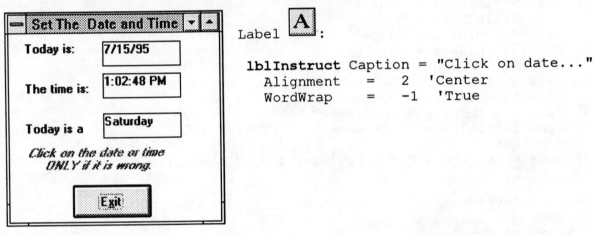

```
lblInstruct Caption = "Click on date..."
   Alignment   =   2   'Center
   WordWrap    =  -1   'True
```

Note: Setting the date and time can lead to errors. Notice the IF statements in the code below to make sure that the user has entered a valid date or time before making the change.

② **Write the Code:** *The code for* **form_load**, **cmd_Exit**, *and* **tmrTimer_Timer** *are the same as above: they are not shown here. Message boxes and input boxes are shown with the code:*

```
Sub lblDay_Click () 'User clicked day of week
   MsgBox "You can not change day of week", 0, "Day of Week"
End Sub
```

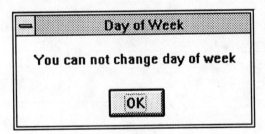

```
Sub lblDate_Click ()
Dim Default, msg, NewDate    ' Declare variables.
 msg = "Enter a new date in the form mm-dd-yyyy"
 Default = Date   ' Current date.
 NewDate = InputBox(msg, "", Default)    ' Get user input.
 If IsDate(NewDate) Then    ' Check if valid.
   Date = NewDate   ' Set date.
   lblDate = Date
 Else
   msg = "You did not enter a valid date, Date NOT reset."
   MsgBox msg, 0, "Set Date"
 End If
 showDay (Now)
End Sub

Sub lblToday_Click () 'Use procedure above if user clicks here
   lblDate_Click
End Sub
```

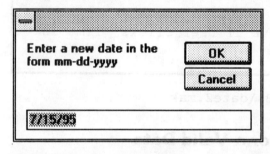
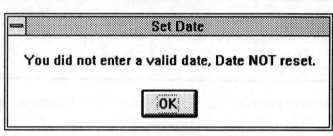

```
Sub lbltime_Click ()
 Dim msg, NewTime    ' Declare variables.
 msg = "Enter a new time in the form hh:mm:ss"
 NewTime = InputBox(msg, "Time", Time)    ' Get user input.
 If Len(NewTime) > 0 Then    ' Check if  valid.
   Time = NewTime   ' Set time.
   lblTime = Time
 Else
   msg = "You did not enter a valid time: Time NOT reset."
   MsgBox msg, 0, "Set Time"
 End If
End Sub
```

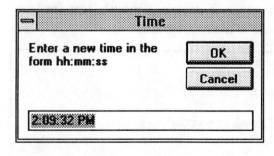
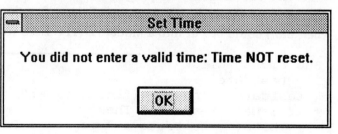

```
Sub showDay (d)    'Receives Date to show Day of week
Dim daynum, msg, valid ' Declare variables.
    If IsDate(d) Then  'Check if valid date
        daynum = Weekday(d)    'Get day of the week: an integer.
      Select Case daynum
        Case 1: lblDay = "Sunday"
        Case 2: lblDay = "Monday"
        Case 3: lblDay = "Tuesday"
        Case 4: lblDay = "Wednesday"
        Case 5: lblDay = "Thursday"
        Case 6: lblDay = "Friday"
        Case 7: lblDay = "Saturday"
      End Select
    Else
        msg = d & " Invalid Date"
        MsgBox msg, 0, "Error"
    End If 'is valid date
End Sub

Sub lblTimeIs_Click ()'Use procedure above if user clicks "Time Is"
   lbltime_Click
End Sub
```

③ **Save the file** as `B:\date2.frm`, save the project as `B:\date2.mak`

Find the Day of the Week for a Valid Date

① **Start a new project, and build the form as shown:**

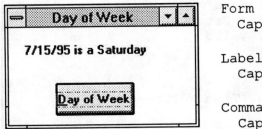

```
Form frmDay:
   Caption = "Day of Week"

Label [A] lblDay:
   Caption = " "

CommandButton [O] cmdDay:
   Caption = "&Day of Week"
```

② **Write the Code:** This program uses the same DayofWeek function shown earlier in this chapter (not shown here). A group of these functions (number of days in a month, test for leap year, etc.) could be put into a module DATE.BAS for reuse in many programs.

```
Sub cmdDay_Click ()
Dim testdate
   testdate = InputBox("Enter date:", "Date", Date)
   If IsDate(testdate) Then
      lblDay = testdate & " is a " & DayOfWeek(testdate)
   Else lblDay = testdate & " Invalid Date"
   End If
End Sub
```

③ **Save the file** as `B:\day_week.frm`, save the project as `B:\day_week.mak`

Error Handling

The program to allow the user to set the system date must consider that the user can enter an invalid date. In the next chapter, we will open files, save files and print. All of these events have the potential to create run time errors: The user selects the B drive with no disk; the printer is off-line, etc. The set date procedure is used to illustrate three methods for handling an invalid entry are shown below, in order of preference:

Method #1: Avoid the Error

```
Sub showDay (d)    'Receives Date to show Day of week
Dim daynum, msg, valid ' Declare variables.
    If IsDate(d) Then  'Check if valid date
        daynum = Weekday(d)    'Get day of the week: an integer.
        Select Case daynum
          Case 1: lblDay = "Sunday"
          Case 2: lblDay = "Monday"
          Case 3: lblDay = "Tuesday"
          Case 4: lblDay = "Wednesday"
          Case 5: lblDay = "Thursday"
          Case 6: lblDay = "Friday"
          Case 7: lblDay = "Saturday"
        End Select
    Else
        msg = d & " Invalid Date"
        MsgBox msg, 0, "Error"
    End If 'is valid date
End Sub
```

Method #2: Resume Next If an Error Occurs

```
Sub showDay (d)    'Receives Date to show Day of week
Dim daynum, msg
    On Error Resume Next  'Keep going if there is an error
    daynum = Weekday(d)    'Causes an error if d is not a valid date.
    If Err = 0 Then    'If d was valid there is no err, err=0
        Select Case daynum
          Case 1: lblDay = "Sunday"
          Case 2: lblDay = "Monday"
          Case 3: lblDay = "Tuesday"
          Case 4: lblDay = "Wednesday"
          Case 5: lblDay = "Thursday"
          Case 6: lblDay = "Friday"
          Case 7: lblDay = "Saturday"
        End Select
    Else
        msg = d & " Invalid Date"
        MsgBox msg, 0, "Error"
    End If 'is valid date
End Sub
```

Method #3: GoTo An Error Handler *(Use GoTo as an absolute last resort!)*

```
Sub showDay (d)    'Receives Date to show Day of week
Dim daynum, msg, valid ' Declare variables.
    On Error GoTo ErrMsg
    daynum = Weekday(d)    'Get day of the week: an integer.
    Select Case daynum
      Case 1: lblDay = "Sunday"
      Case 2: lblDay = "Monday"
      Case 3: lblDay = "Tuesday"
      Case 4: lblDay = "Wednesday"
      Case 5: lblDay = "Thursday"
      Case 6: lblDay = "Friday"
      Case 7: lblDay = "Saturday"
    End Select
    Exit Sub    'Exit before getting to the error handler
ErrMsg:
    msg = d & " Invalid Date"
    MsgBox msg, 0, "Error"
    Resume Next    'Still need resume
End Sub
```

Chapter 9

Importing

Use
Common Dialog
Boxes to
Select Font
&
Color

Use File Controls

OLE!
Object Linking
&
Embedding

Dialog Boxes

Visual Basic can access Windows *Common Dialog Boxes*. Two that you may have seen frequently are the *Font Dialog Box* and the *Color Dialog Box*. The "Happy Birthday" program uses both of these dialog boxes to create a Birthday Card. The *Select Printer Dialog Box* can be opened before printing the form.

The "Happy Birthday" program at run time, after the fonts and colors have changed.

① **Build the form** as shown below, Change the names and captions as shown:

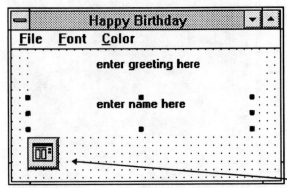

```
Form frmHappy
    AutoRedraw  = -1  'True
    Caption     = "Happy Birthday"

TextBoxes [ab]:
    txtGreeting, txtfriend
    Alignment   = 2  'Center
    BorderStyle = 0  'None
    MultiLine   = -1  'True
    Text = "type greeting/name here"
CommonDialog: CMDialog1
```

Note: If you do not see the Common Dialog Control, 🔲 on your toolbox, you must add it :
   ① A: Select **Files**, **Add File...**
   ① B: Select the file C:\WINDOWS\SYSTEM\CMDIALOG.VBX

---

② **Build the Menu** 📋 according to the table below:

Caption	Name	
&File	mnuFile	
&Select Printer	mnuSelect	
&Print	mnuPrint	
-	mnuSep1	'draws a line on the menu
E&xit	mnuExit	
&Font	mnuFont	
&Greeting	mnuFontGreeting	
&Name	mnuFontName	
&Color	mnuColor	
&Greeting	mnuColorGreeting	
&Name	mnuColorName	

③ Write the Code:

```
Sub Form_Load () 'Different confetti each time it runs
 Randomize
End Sub

Sub confetti ()   'A general procedure
Dim c, x, y, Color
 For c = 1 To 200                'Sprinkle 200 pieces of Confetti
    x = Int(Rnd * scalewidth)    'any column on form
    y = Int(Rnd * scaleheight)   'any row on form
    Color = Int(Rnd * 15) + 1    'No black confetti
    Line (x, y)-(x + 30, y + 30), QBColor(Color), BF
 Next c
End Sub

Sub Form_Activate () 'Confetti is erased when font or color changes
 confetti            're-draw the confetti
End Sub

Sub mnuColorName_Click ()            'Change color of the name
  Call selectColor(txtFriend)
End Sub

Sub mnuColorGreeting_Click ()    'Change color of the greeting
  Call selectColor(txtGreeting)
End Sub

Sub selectColor (txt As TextBox) 'Receives text box to change
  CMDialog1.Action = 3 'Open color Dialog Window
  'After the color dialog window closes, use the values:
  txt.ForeColor = CMDialog1.Color 'Change the color of text box
End Sub
```

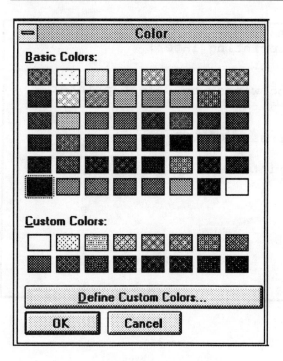

When the user selects color from the menu, the mnuColor_Click procedure opens the Common dialog Color window. After the user selects a color, the dialog window closes and the color of the text is changed to the color property of the Common Dialog control.

```
Sub mnuFontName_Click ()         'Change the font on the name
   Call selectFont(txtFriend)
End Sub

Sub mnuFontGreeting_Click () 'Change the font on the greeting
   Call selectFont(txtGreeting)
End Sub

Sub selectFont (txt As TextBox) 'Receive text box to change
   CMDialog1.Flags = &H1& 'Select screen fonts only
   CMDialog1.Action = 4     'Open Font Dialog Window
   'After the font dialog window closes, use the values:
   txt.FontSize = CMDialog1.FontSize       'Change text box received
   txt.FontBold = CMDialog1.FontBold
   txt.FontItalic = CMDialog1.FontItalic
   txt.FontName = CMDialog1.FontName
End Sub
```

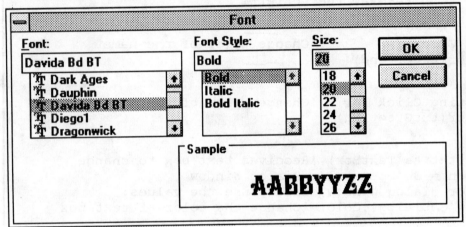

The fonts that appear in the font dialog box will probably be different on your computer.

The flag setting lists only those screen fonts supported by your system.

For more information, select Help in Visual Basic and search for Font Dialog, Flags.

```
Sub mnuPrint_Click ()   'Print the form
   PrintForm    'Easy printing, more on printing later!
End Sub

Sub mnuSelect_Click () 'Open the dialog window to select printer
   'Don't crash if the printer is off
   On Error Resume Next
   'Treat it as an error if the user presses CANCEL
   CMDialog1.CancelError = True
   'Set flags for printer setup (not print)
   CMDialog1.Flags = &H40&
   'Display the print setup window
   CMDialog1.Action = 5
End Sub

Sub mnuExit_Click () 'End program
   End
End Sub
```

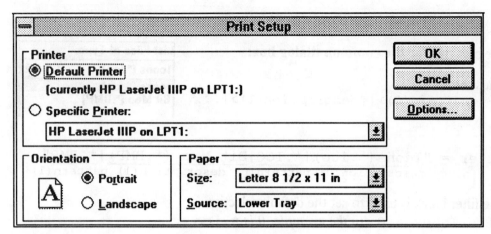

You do not need to include the select printer command if you have just one printer, but you should put it in anyway - in case you get a color printer or give the program to someone else.

④ **Save the project** as B:\birthday.frm, B:\birthday.mak

Common Dialog to Select File

This program uses the Common Dialog to view icons. After you write this program, you can go back to the Birthday Program and use the same method to pick a picture to the birthday card. (If you make changes to the Birthday program save it as a different name - the birthday program is used later in the book.) *Opening files can cause errors, notice the error checking in this program.*

① **Build the Form**, change the names, captions and properties as shown:

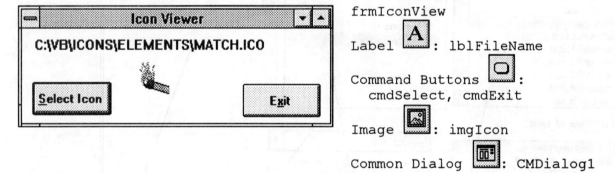

```
Sub cmdSelect_Click ()
 On Error Resume Next    'Opening files can cause errors
 cmDialog1.Filter = "Icons (*.ico)|*.ICO|Bit Map (*.BMP)|*.BMP"
 cmDialog1.FilterIndex = 0  'Icons (*.ico)
 cmDialog1.Action = 1     'Open file dialog window
 If Err = 0 Then          'After selection, if no error load picture
  imgIcon.Picture=LoadPicture(cmDialog1.Filename)'load selected file
  lblFileName.Caption = cmDialog1.Filename 'Display name of file
 End If
End Sub

Sub cmdExit_Click ()
 End
End Sub
```

② **Write the Code:**

③ **Save the file** as `B:\icon.frm`, save the project as `B:\icon.mak`

An explanation of the settings for the common dialog box:

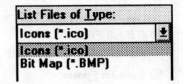

FILTER: The filter must be:
<description(0)>|<pattern(0)>|<description(1)>|...

`Example:`
```
cmDialog1.Filter = "Icons(*.ico)|*.ICO|Bit Map (*.BMP)|*.BMP"
```
                      description(0) pattern(0) description(1) pattern(1)

FILTER INDEX: The filter index is used to set the default selection:
```
cmDialog1.FilterIndex = 0
```
'In the example, 0 is `*.ico`

The File Controls

The common dialog control is convenient is you want to open a single file. If you want to view several files, it can be irritating to have the *open dialog* window popping up and then closing. This program uses the drive list, directory list, and file list controls to view pictures.

① **Build the Form**:

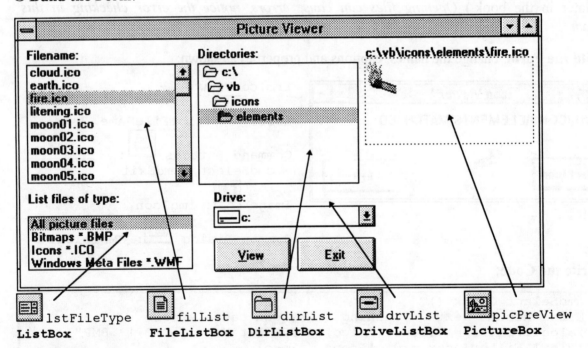

② **Change the Properties:**

The **FileListBox** filList, **DriveListBox** drvList, and **DirListBox** dirList *do not need to have any properties changed.*

Form: `frmPicView`
   Caption   = "Picture Viewer"
   Icon   *select an icon after you run the program*

ListBox: `lstFileType`
   Text   = " "

PictureBox: picPreView

    AutoSize   = True   *(allows display of any size picture)*
    BorderStyle   = *None*

CommandButtons:
cmdPreView
    Caption   = "&View"
cmdExit
    Caption   = "E&xit"

Labels:
lblPreview
    Caption   = " "
    AutoSize   = True *(allows display of any size filename)*
lblFilename
    Caption   = "Filename:"
lblDirectory
    Caption   = "Directories:"
lblDrive
    Caption   = "Drive:"
lblFileType
    Caption   = "List files of type:"

③ **Write the Code:**

```
Sub drvList_Change () 'Trying to change drives can cause error
  On Error Resume Next
  dirList.Path = drvList.Drive
  If Err <> 0 Then MsgBox Error(Err), 48, "Error" 'Message if error
End Sub

Sub Form_Load ()
'Add file types to combo box, initialize file list pattern
  lstFileType.AddItem "All picture files"        'Item 0
  lstFileType.AddItem "Bitmaps *.BMP"            'Item 1
  lstFileType.AddItem "Icons *.ICO"              'Item 2
  lstFileType.AddItem "Windows Meta Files *.WMF" 'Item 3
  lstFileType.ListIndex = 0                      'Default is Item 0
  'Moves item 0, All Picture Files, to text window
  filList.Pattern = "*.BMP;*.ICO;*.WMF"  'Use ; to separate types
End Sub

Sub lstFileType_Change () 'User selected a file type
'User has selected type of file, change pattern for file list box:
  Select Case lstFileType.ListIndex  'List index is item selected
    Case 0   'Selected All picture Files
      filList.Pattern = "*.BMP;*.ICO;*.WMF"
    Case 1   'Selected Bitmap Files
      filList.Pattern = "*.BMP"
    Case 2   'Selected Icons
      filList.Pattern = "*.ICO"
    Case 3   'Selected Windows Meta Files
      filList.Pattern = "*.WMF"
  End Select
```

```
    filList.Path = dirList.Path   'Update the list
End Sub

Sub lstFileType_Click ()
  lstFileType_Change     'Use procedure above for either action
End Sub

Sub dirList_Change ()
  filList.Path = dirList.Path
End Sub

Sub filList_DblClick ()'double clicking filename previews picture
  cmdPreview_Click
End Sub

Sub cmdPreview_Click () 'concatenate path and filename, then display
Dim File
  If filList.ListIndex >= 0 Then
    File = filList.Path
    'Make sure the path ends in \ Right$ is used to look at last letter
    If Right$(File, 1) <> "\" Then File = File & "\"
    'Add the filename to get complete file definition
    File = File & filList.List(filList.ListIndex)
  End If
  lblPreview.Caption = File  'Show the complete filename
  picPreView.Picture = LoadPicture(File) 'Load the picture
End Sub

Sub cmdExit_Click () 'Start with something familiar: ending!
  End                      'End the program
End Sub
```

④ **Save the file** as `B:\picture.frm`, save the project as `B:\picture.mak`

OLE: Object Linking and Embedding

The "Happy New Year" program is similar to the Happy Birthday program, but uses OLE, (object linking and embedding). An OLE control can be linked to other applications such as the Microsoft Word Art Application, or the Paint Program. When the user clicks on the OLE object, the Word Art, or other application, is launched. The user can then embed text in several different styles and Paintbrush pictures into the greeting card.

Note: If you do not see the OLE control, on your toolbar, you must add it :
   ① **A:** Select **Files, Add File...**
   ① **B:** Select the file `C:\WINDOWS\SYSTEM\MSOLE2.VBX`

---

① **Start a new project**. Name the form frmNewYear, change the caption to "Happy New Year".

② **Click on the OLE Control** 🖳 : When you click on the OLE control, the _Insert Object_ window shown below opens. The choice of objects to insert depends on what software is loaded on your machine. The WordArt and PaintBrush applications are included with Windows.

③ **Select Paintbrush Picture** and press OK.

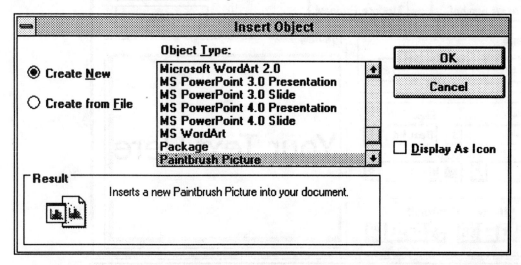

The Painbrush Picture application is started immediately: you can draw an appropriate picture for New Years. Whatever you draw now is what the user sees when he starts _your_ application. (If you really don't want to try your hand as an artist, select the text tool and write "Double-Click here to draw a picture."

② **Click on the OLE Control** 🖳 again, this time select Microsoft WordArt. The WordArt application allows you to enter text, then stretch, it curve it, add shadows and create other effects. You can make changes now, or leave as is. Any changes you make now the user will see when the program starts.

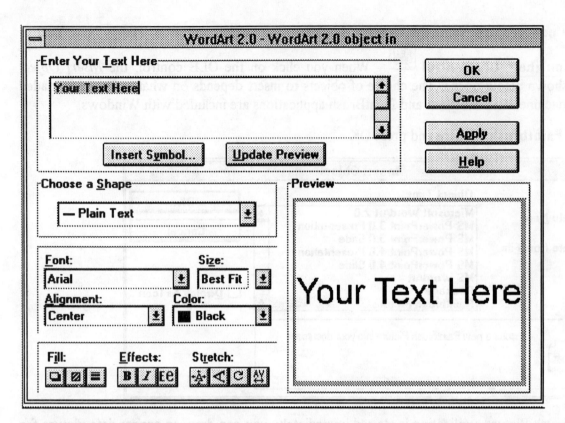

The Form: There are no other controls on the form. The form will look about the same at design time as at run time. At run time the user can click on the word art or the paintbrush picture to make change. Changes made at run time are not permanent. The next time the program runs the picture and text entered at design time will reappear. (The user can save any picture he draws while in the paintbrush application.)

Stretch the size of the embedded objects at design time.

There is no code, no properties to change for the "New Year" program. However, you will probably want to add a menu to **Exit, Select Printer** and **Print** exactly as in the "Birthday" program.

③ **Save the file** as B:\newyear.frm, save the project as B:\newyear.mak

Chapter 10

Combo Boxes: Print & Save

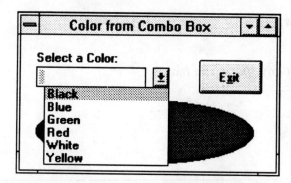

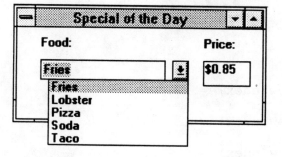

Learn About the Combo Box:

Add & Delete

Print

Save

Save As

The Combo Box

The Combo Box ⊞ is similar to the list box ⊞ . The main differences are:

- A combo box combines a piece of information (itemdata) with each item in the box.

- The list box could be stretched bigger, the combo box is always a drop down list.

The "Combo Color" Program

This program uses a combo box to select QBColor.

① **Start a new project and build the form using the names and captions shown below:**

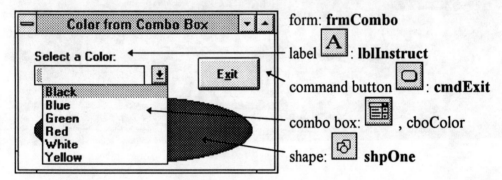

form: **frmCombo**

label **A** : **lblInstruct**

command button ⊡ : **cmdExit**

combo box: ⊞ , cboColor

shape: ⊡ **shpOne**

② **Change the properties as shown below:**

shape **shpOne**:
    fillStyle   = solid, *make it any shape you like.*
combo box **cboColor**:
    sorted   = true
    Text   = " "

③ **Add the code:**

```
Sub cmdExit_Click ()
  End
End Sub

Sub Form_Load ()
  cboColor.AddItem "Red"
  cboColor.ItemData(cboColor.NewIndex) = 12
  cboColor.AddItem "Blue"
  cboColor.ItemData(cboColor.NewIndex) = 1
  cboColor.AddItem "Black"
  cboColor.ItemData(cboColor.NewIndex) = 0
  cboColor.AddItem "Green"
  cboColor.ItemData(cboColor.NewIndex) = 10
  cboColor.AddItem "White"
  cboColor.ItemData(cboColor.NewIndex) = 15
  cboColor.AddItem "Yellow"
  cboColor.ItemData(cboColor.NewIndex) = 14
End Sub
```

```
Sub cboColor_Click ()
  Dim color
  color = cboColor.ItemData(cboColor.ListIndex)
  shpOne.FillColor = QBColor(color)
End Sub
```

When an item is selected from a combo box, listindex is the index of the selected item. When an item is added to a combo box, newindex is the index of the new item. When an item is assigned an itemdata, the itemdata stays with the item even if a new entry changes the index of the item. (The "List Box Color" program could not sort the names in the list, because without itemdata the only way to tell the color was the index in the list.)

④ **Save the file** as B:\clr_cbo.frm, save the project as B:\clr_cbo.mak

The "Special of the Day" Program

This program uses a combo box to list menu items and prices. For example, there might be an item 'hot-dog' in the list. The price can be stored as the itemdata. The item data must be an integer, but we can store the price as 125 instead of $1.25. The program divides the number by 100 before it displays it.

① **Start a new project and build the form:** frmSpecial

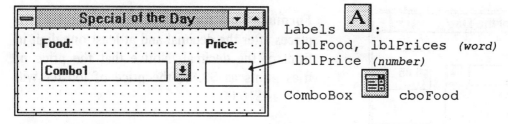

Labels A:
   lblFood, lblPrices *(word)*
   lblPrice *(number)*

ComboBox   cboFood

② **Change the Properties:**

```
Form frmSpecial:
   Caption           = "Special of the Day"
ComboBox cboFood:
   Sorted            = -1   'True
   Text              = " "
Label lblPrices:
   Caption           = "Price:"
Label lblFood:
   Caption           = "Food:"
Label lblPrice:
   BorderStyle       = 1    'Fixed Single
```

③ Write the Code:

```
Sub Form_Load ()    'Prices are multiplied by 100
  cboFood.AddItem "Pizza"
  cboFood.ItemData(cboFood.NewIndex) = 135
  cboFood.AddItem "Fries"
  cboFood.ItemData(cboFood.NewIndex) = 85
  cboFood.AddItem "Soda"
  cboFood.ItemData(cboFood.NewIndex) = 70
  cboFood.AddItem "Taco"
  cboFood.ItemData(cboFood.NewIndex) = 225
  cboFood.AddItem "Lobster"
  cboFood.ItemData(cboFood.NewIndex) = 1000
  cboFood.ListIndex = 0
End Sub

Sub cboFood_Click () 'Food selected: display price
Dim Price
  'Price is the item data of item selected, divided by 100:
  Price = cboFood.ItemData(cboFood.ListIndex)/100
  'Format to force 2 places after decimal and at least 1 before
  lblPrice = Format(Price, "$##0.00")
End Sub
```

At run time the items are sorted in alphabetic order:

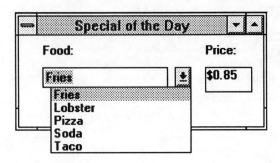

Format: The format **$##0.00** forces two places after the decimal and at least one digit in front of the decimal. Notice that the price of fries prints as $0.85, the price of lobster will print as $10.00.

④ Save the file as B:\special.frm, save the project as B:\special.mak

Add, Delete and Change

The 'Special of the Day' program will now be modified to allow the user to add and delete items from the combo box at run time. Changes made at run time are not permanent: if you add an item, or change the price, the new information will not be there the next time you run the program. Modifications to save the changes are added in the next section.

① **Load the "Special of the Day" program:** `special.mak`

The only change to the form is to make it wider in order for the menu to fit:

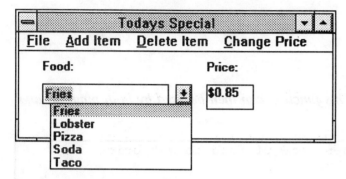

② **Create the Menu according to the table below:**

Caption	Name	ShortCut Key
&File	mnuFile	
&Save	mnuSave	Ctrl + S
-	mnuSep1	
&Print	mnuPrint	Ctrl + P
-	mnuSep2	
E&xit	mnuExit	
&Add Item	mnuAdd	
&Delete Item	mnuDelete	
&Change Price	mnuChange	

It is important to check for invalid numbers when the user is asked to enter a price. A common mistake is for the user to enter a $. The user is not asked to multiply by 100, they enter the number with a decimal place and the program multiplies it by 100.

③ **Modify the Code:**

```
Sub mnuAdd_Click ()
Dim Food, price, msg
  Food = InputBox("Name of Food: ", "Add Food")
  If Food <> "" Then  'User did not press cancel
    msg = "Enter price of " & Food
    price = getPrice(Food)
    If price <> -1 Then
      cboFood.AddItem Food
      cboFood.ItemData(cboFood.NewIndex) = price * 100
      mnuDelete.Enabled = True  'There is something to delete now
      cboFood.ListIndex = cboFood.NewIndex 'Select new item
    End If
  End If
End Sub
```

A function is used to return the new price. This function can then be used by both mnuAdd and mnuChange.

```
Function getPrice (Food) 'receives name of food to ask price
  Dim msg, price
  msg = "Enter price of " & Food
  Do
     price = InputBox(msg, "Price") 'Shown below
     'If user presses cancel, signal to cancel, allow loop to end
     If price = "" Then price = -1
     If Not IsNumeric(price) Then 'change msg and re-do
        msg = "Not a valid number: please enter price of " & Food
     End If
  Loop Until IsNumeric(price)
  getPrice = price   'return price to calling procedure
End Function
```

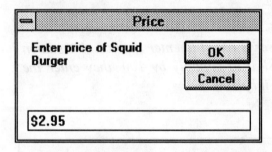

④ **Save before continuing.**

```
Sub mnuChange_Click ()
Dim price, Food
  Food = cboFood.Text
  price = getPrice(Food)   ' -1 signals cancel
  If price <> -1 Then
    cboFood.ItemData(cboFood.ListIndex) = price * 100
    lblPrice = Format(price, "$##0.00")
  End If
End Sub

Sub mnuDelete_Click ()
Dim ans, msg
  msg = "Delete " & cboFood.Text
  ans = MsgBox(msg, 1, "Delete")
  If ans = 1 Then 'User selected OK
    cboFood.RemoveItem cboFood.ListIndex
    If cboFood.ListCount = 0 Then
      'If nothing in list, disable delete to prevent crash!
      mnuDelete.Enabled = False
    Else
      cboFood.ListIndex = 0 'Display first item in list
    End If
  End If
End Sub

Sub mnuExit_Click () 'End program
  End
End Sub
```

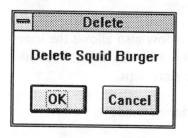

Maybe squid burgers didn't sell as well as the market research team predicted.

Save before continuing.

Error Checks

The program avoids two types of errors that could cause this program to crash:

The user could enter an invalid price: $2.95 instead of 2.95, for example.

- If the price is not a number: **If Not IsNumeric(price)**; the message is changed and the user is asked to try again until they enter a valid number, or press CANCEL.

If the user clicks delete when there is nothing in the list, or nothing selected, the program would crash.

- When an item is deleted, the first item is selected and moved into the text area: **cboFood.ListIndex = 0**

- When the last item is deleted from the list: `listCount =0` the delete command is disabled `mnuDelete.Enabled = False`

- When an item is added, the delete command is enabled: `mnuDelete.Enabled = True`

Printing

The "Special of the Day" program allows the user to add, delete and change the prices of items. The next step is to print the menu on paper: There are a number of printer properties that can be changed, this program illustrates:

- `Printer.FontBold = True`   'Print bold headings

- `Printer.NewPage`   'Each menu is printed on a new page

- `Printer.EndDoc`   'The printer is released at the end

- `Printer.Print`   'Print a blank line

```
    MENU

FOOD          PRICE
Fries         $  0.85
Lobster       $10.00
Pizza         $  1.35
Soda          $  0.70
Taco          $  2.25
```

Printer.FontBold = True
printer.print for blank line
Printer.FontBold = False after printing this line
If statement & format$ to line up numbers.

Printer.NewPage after last line,
Printer.EndDoc after last copy.

The user can select a printer, and number of copies. The print dialog window also allows the user to select page numbers, but this program ignores those selections. To add this feature to the program, calculate the number of lines per page and the item number to start with.

① **Add the Common Dialog control** to the form (for the print dialog window)

② **Add the Code:** (We already added print to the menu)

```
Sub mnuPrint_Click ()
Dim item, price, copy
  On Error Resume Next
  CMDialog1.CancelError = True 'treat cancel as an error
  CMDialog1.Action = 5
  If Err = 0 Then
    For copy = 1 To CMDialog1.Copies    'User can select # of copies
      printer.FontBold = True           'Make heading in bold
      printer.Print "   MENU"           'Print heading
      printer.Print                     'Print a blank line
      printer.Print "FOOD", "PRICE"     'Print sub-heading
      printer.FontBold = False          'Turn off bold
      'Print each item: if listcount is 3, items are 0, 1 and 2
      For item = 0 To cboFood.ListCount - 1
        price = cboFood.ItemData(item) / 100
        printer.Print cboFood.List(item),
```

```
        If price >= 10 Then
            printer.Print Format$(price, "$00.00")
        Else printer.Print Format$(price, "$ 0.00")
        End If
    Next item
    printer.NewPage    'Each menu on a new page
  Next copy
  printer.EndDoc       'Release the printer
  End If
End Sub
```

④ **Save before continuing.**

SAVE the SQUID!

The "Special of the Day" program is not finished yet. After adding squid burgers and raising the price on lobster, the user will want to save the file!

The contents of the combo box are saved by writing each item in the combo box and its itemdata to a random access file.

All of the records in a random access file must be exactly the same length. In order to create records that are exactly the same length, we must define the record in a module.

① **Add a new module to the project:** From the menu select **File, New Module**. The new module is given a default name of MODULE1.BAS. The file can be given a different name when it is saved.

② **Add the following code to MODULE1.BAS:**

```
Option Explicit
Type FoodType
  FoodName As String * 15 'FoodName can have no more than 15 letters
  Price As Double          'Price is a number with decimal places
End Type
```

When the file is created, each record will take exactly the same amount of space:

| Fries□□□□□□□□□□00.85 | Lobster□□□□□□□□10.00 | Pizza□□□□□□□□□□□01.35 |

The file can be read in random order by multiplying the size of a record by the record number to get the address where a particular record is stored. This program does not use random access, it reads the records sequentially.

One trick that is used if you want to save more than one piece of information is to read the file sequentially, making itemdata the record number. When an item from the combo box is selected, retrieve the record using the itemdata (record number). This method is not shown, because it is easier to create a database. (Databases are covered in chapter 14.)

Variables can now be declared as FoodType. The statement **Dim Food as FoodType** declares Food to have two parts: **Food.FoodName** and **Food.Price**. We can assign values or print the parts of FoodType just like other variables:

```
Food.FoodName ="Pizza"
If Food.Price > 10  then ...
```

③ Modify the Code:

Instead of adding the five items and prices as constants, form_load will open the file and read all of the records in the file. Each record will be added to the combo box as before. The first time you run the program, there will not be any records in the file and the combo box will be empty after form load. *(To avoid an empty list the first time, add the mnuSave procedure first, run the program, then modify the form_load procedure.)*

```
Sub mnuSave_click ()
Dim fooditem As FoodType
Dim count
  On Error Resume Next
  Kill "FOOD.BAK"                  'Remove old backup
  Name "FOOD.DTA" As "FOOD.BAK"   'The current one is now backup
  Open "FOOD.DTA" For Random As #1 Len = Len(fooditem)
  For count = 0 To cboFood.ListCount - 1
    fooditem.foodname = cboFood.List(count)
    fooditem.price = cboFood.ItemData(count) / 100
    Put #1, count + 1, fooditem
  Next count
  Close #1
End Sub
```

Run the program once at this point to avoid an empty list.

```
Sub Form_Load ()
Dim fooditem As FoodType
Dim count
  On Error Resume Next
  Open "FOOD.DTA" For Random As #1 Len = Len(fooditem)
  count = 1
  While Not EOF(1)
    Get #1, count, fooditem
    If Not EOF(1) Then
      cboFood.AddItem fooditem.foodname
      cboFood.ItemData(cboFood.NewIndex) = fooditem.price * 100
    End If
    count = count + 1
  Wend
  Close (1)
  cboFood.ListIndex = 0
End Sub
```

The mnuExit procedure is modified to ask the user if they want to save before exiting. If the user answers yes, the procedure mnuSave is called. If the answer is No, the program ends. If they press cancel, no code is executed. (No code is needed to 'do nothing'.)

```
Sub mnuExit_Click ()
Dim ans
 ans = MsgBox("Do you want to save?", 3, "Quit?")
 Select Case ans
    Case 6:           'Yes
       mnuSave_click  'save first, then end
       End
    Case 7: End       'No
 End Select           'Do NOT do anything if they selected cancel
End Sub
```

Save before continuing.

SAVE AS

Form_Load always opens and saves the same file. It is possible that the user would like to create several different menus. The next modification is to allow the user to select Open, Save and Save As from the menu. The common dialog control is used to select the file name to open and save.

① **Change the text property of the combo box to " "**

② **Modify the Menu according to the table below:**

Caption	Name	ShortCut Key
&File	mnuFile	
&New	mnuNew	
&Open	mnuOpen	Ctrl + O
&Save	mnuSave	Ctrl + S
Save &As	mnuSaveAs	Ctrl + A
-	mnuSep1	
&Print	mnuPrint	Ctrl + P
-	mnuSep2	
E&xit	mnuExit	
&Add Item	mnuAdd	
&Delete Item	mnuDelete	
&Change Price	mnuChange	

② **Modify the Code:**

The procedure mnuSaveAs is added to let the user select a file, then write the file in mnuSave:

```
Sub mnuSaveAs_Click ()
  On Error Resume Next
  CMDialog1.CancelError = True 'treat cancel as an error
  CMDialog1.DialogTitle = "Save File"
  CMDialog1.Filter = "Data Files|*.DTA"
  CMDialog1.Action = 2           'Save File
  If Err = 0 Then mnuSave_Click
End Sub
```

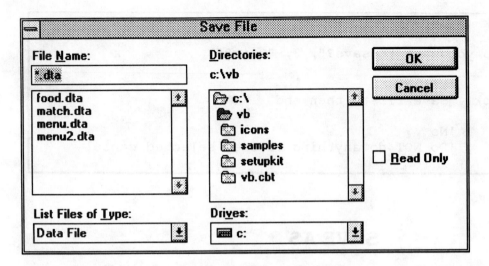

After a file is selected, the CMDialog1.FileName property has the name of the file selected.

```
Sub mnuSave_Click ()
Dim fooditem As FoodType
Dim count
  On Error Resume Next
  If CMDialog1.FileName = "" Then mnuSaveAs_Click 'Get a name
  Open CMDialog1.Filename For Random As #1 Len = Len(fooditem)
  For count = 0 To cboFood.ListCount - 1
    fooditem.foodname = cboFood.List(count)
    fooditem.price = cboFood.ItemData(count) / 100
    Put #1, count + 1, fooditem
  Next count
  Close #1
End Sub
```

When the user selects Exit, the program asks if they want to save. If they answer Yes, the Save As procedure is called to let them select a file.

```
Sub mnuExit_Click ()
Dim ans
  ans = MsgBox("Do you want to save?", 3, "Quit?")
  Select Case ans
    Case 6:            'Yes
      mnuSaveAs_Click  'save first, then end
      End
    Case 7: End        'No
  End Select           'Do NOT do anything if they selected cancel
End Sub
```

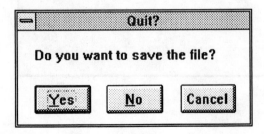

There should be no code in Form_Load: delete all of it. The combo box will be empty until the user selects File, Open.

```
Sub mnuOpen_Click ()
Dim fooditem As FoodType
Dim count
  mnuNew_Click 'mnuNew asks if they want to save first & clears
  On Error Resume Next
  CMDialog1.CancelError = True 'treat cancel as an error
  CMDialog1.DialogTitle = "Open File"
  CMDialog1.Filter = "Data Files|*.DTA"
  CMDialog1.Action = 1            'Open File
  If Err = 0 Then
    Open CMDialog1.Filename For Random As #1 Len = Len(fooditem)
    count = 1
    While Not EOF(1)
      Get #1, count, fooditem
      If Not EOF(1) Then
        cboFood.AddItem fooditem.foodname
        cboFood.ItemData(cboFood.NewIndex) = fooditem.price * 100
      End If
      count = count + 1
    Wend
    Close (1)
    cboFood.ListIndex = 0
  Else MsgBox "Unable to Open File", 0, "File ERROR"
  End If
  If cboFood.ListCount <= 0 Then
    mnuDelete.Enabled = False
  Else
    mnuDelete.Enabled = True
  End If
End Sub
```

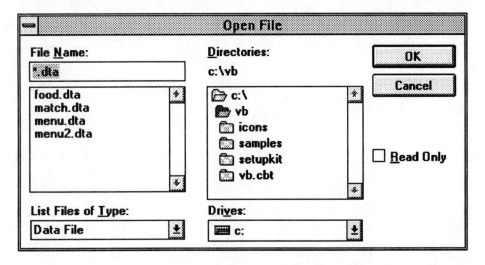

```
Sub mnuNew_Click ()
Dim ans
  If cboFood.ListCount > 0 Then
    ans = MsgBox("Do you want to save the file?", 3, "Save")
  End If
  If ans = 6 Then mnuSaveAs_click   '6 is Yes
  If (ans = 6) Or (ans = 7) Then    '7 is No
    cboFood.Clear    'Erase everything in combo box
    mnuDelete.Enabled = False
  End If
End Sub
```

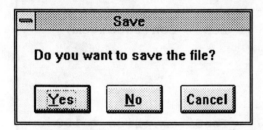

Yes! Save the file - The "Special of the Day" program is complete.

Chapter 11

The Grid Control

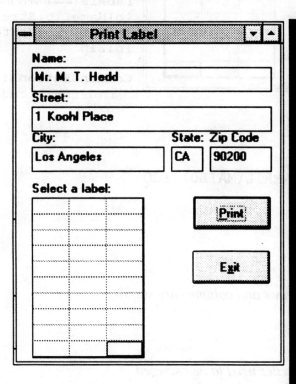

Use the Grid Control:

Select Row & Column

Add & Delete

Create a Weekly Schedule

Use Nested Loops to Print Hours & Minutes

Printing Labels

One type of labels comes on sheets with three columns and ten rows. If you use this kind of label, you may have a sheet of labels with only a few labels left on the sheet. The "Labels" program uses a grid to let the user select which label on the sheet to print. When the user selects PRINT, a FOR loop prints the number of lines necessary to move to the selected row, then TAB is used to move to the selected column. The program prints name and addresses, but the program could be changed to accommodate any kind of information, and other size labels. The diagram shows the last label on the page selected.

① Build the Form:

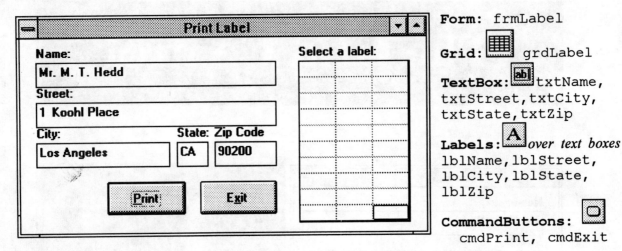

Form: `frmLabel`

Grid: `grdLabel`

TextBox: `txtName, txtStreet, txtCity, txtState, txtZip`

Labels: *over text boxes* `lblName, lblStreet, lblCity, lblState, lblZip`

CommandButtons: `cmdPrint, cmdExit`

② Change the Properties:

```
Form frmLabel
   Caption       = "Print Label"
   Icon          = C:\VB\ICONS\MAIL\MAIL01.ICO

Grid grdLabel
   Cols          = 3
   FixedCols     = 0
   FixedRows     = 0
   Rows          = 10
```
Adjust the width and height so that all rows and columns are visible.

```
CommandButton cmdExit
   Caption       = "E&xit"
```

CommonDialog CMDialog1 *no properties need to be changed*

```
CommandButton cmdPrint
   Caption       = "&Print"
```

③ Arrange the TabIndex for the following text boxes so that pressing Tab moves to the next box in the following order:

```
txtName (tabIndex = 1), txtStreet (tabIndex = 2),
txtCity(tabIndex = 3), txtState(tabIndex = 4), txtZip(tabIndex = 5)
```

```
Labels:
 lblInstruct
   Caption          = "Select a label:"
 lblZip
   Caption          = "Zip Code"
 lblState
   Caption          = "State:"
lblCity
   Caption          = "City:"
lblStreet
   Caption          = "Street:"
lblName
   Caption          = "Name:"
```

④ **Write The Code:** These particular labels have 1 space on the left edge. There are two rows at the top of the page before the first row of labels begin. Each label is about 27 spaces wide and has 6 lines. The tab for the first label is set to 2, the tab for the second label is set to 29 and the tab for the third label is set to 56. Two lines at the top plus six lines or each row are skipped to print the selected label. Your labels may be different.

```
Sub cmdExit_Click ()
   End
End Sub

Sub cmdPrint_Click ()
Dim x, y
   On Error Resume Next
   'Calculate column to print in, to use for TAB:
   If grdLabel.Col = 0 Then x = 2  'Col 0 of grid = 1st row of labels
   If grdLabel.Col = 1 Then x = 29 'Col 1 of grid = middle row
   If grdLabel.Col = 2 Then x = 56 'Col 2 is last row of labels
   'Print blank lines to move to correct line:
   'These labels have 6 lines per label, and 2 blank lines at top:
   'If row is 0, only 2 blank lines are printed (0*6=0)
   For y = 0 To grdLabel.Row * 6 + 2
      printer.Print   'print nothing, just move to next line
   Next y
   printer.Print Tab(x); txtName
   printer.Print Tab(x); txtStreet
   printer.Print Tab(x); txtCity; ","; txtState; " "; txtZip
   printer.EndDoc
End Sub

Sub Form_Load ()
   grdLabel.Row = 0    'Use first label if user doesn't select one
   grdLabel.Col = 0
End Sub
```

Note: The ASCII character 13 is returned when the user presses ⏎**Enter**. The user should be able to either press ⏎**Enter** or press ⎄**Tab** to move to the next box. The command setFocus is used to change to the next text box. When the user presses ⏎**Enter** after typing the zip code, the focus is set to the print button. *(Use cut and paste to enter similar code 5 times in the next section.)*

```
Sub txtname_KeyPress (keyascii As Integer)    'Move to next box if
   If keyascii = 13 Then txtStreet.SetFocus    '  user presses ENTER
End Sub

Sub txtStreet_KeyPress (keyascii As Integer)'Move to city if
   If keyascii = 13 Then txtCity.SetFocus      '  user presses ENTER
End Sub

Sub txtCity_KeyPress (keyascii As Integer)  'Move to state if
   If keyascii = 13 Then txtState.SetFocus    '  user presses ENTER
End Sub

Sub txtState_KeyPress (keyascii As Integer)'Move to zip code if
   If keyascii = 13 Then txtZip.SetFocus       '  user presses ENTER
End Sub

Sub txtZip_KeyPress (keyascii As Integer)   'Move to print command if
   If keyascii = 13 Then cmdPrint.SetFocus    '  user presses ENTER
End Sub
```

⑤ **Save the file as** B:\label.frm, **save the project as** B:\label.mak.

(This program is modified in chapter 12.)

The Schedule Program

The Schedule Program uses the grid control to print a schedule for the week. Form load puts the day of the week in the column headings and the time in the row headings. The rest of the grid is blank. The user can type a word in the **Item to Add** text box, then highlight a block of cells and press **Add** to put the word in all of the highlighted cells. Text can not be entered directly into the grid.

	Monday	Tuesday	Wednesday	Thursday	Friday	Saturday	Sunday
9AM	coffee	coffee	coffee	coffee	coffee		
10AM	coffee	coffee	coffee	coffee	coffee		
11AM	work	work	work	work	work	coffee	coffee
12AM	lunch	lunch	lunch	lunch	lunch	coffee	coffee
1PM	lunch	lunch	lunch	lunch	lunch	coffee	coffee
2PM	rest	rest	rest	rest	rest	lunch	lunch
3PM						lunch	lunch
4PM							
5PM							
6PM	dinner	dinner	dinner	dinner	dinner	dinner	dinner
7PM	dinner	dinner	dinner	dinner	dinner	dinner	dinner
8PM	dinner	dinner	dinner	dinner	dinner	dinner	dinner
9PM							
10PM							
11PM							

Title bar: **Weekly Schedule**

Menu: **File   Help**

Item to Add:

`rest`

[**Add**]

① **Start a new project, build the form and change the properties:**

Form frmSched
    Caption   = "Weekly Schedule"
    Height   = 5865
    Width   = 8040

TextBox [ab]: txtItem
    Left   = 240
    Text   = " "

CommandButton [O]: cmdAdd
    Caption   = "&Add"

Grid [▦]: grdSched
    Cols   = 8
    Height   = 3975
    Left   = 0
    Rows   = 16
    Top   = 0
    Width   = 7815

Label [A]: lblItem
    Caption   = "Item to Add:"

② **Build the Menu:**

Caption	Name
&File	mnuFile
&Print	mnuPrint
-	mnuSep
E&xit	mnuExit
&Help	mnuHelp

③ **Write the Code:**

```
Sub Form_Load ()
   columnHeading 'label columns Monday, Tuesday, etc.
   rowHeading    'label rows 9AM, 10AM...11PM
End Sub

Sub columnHeading ()    'label columns Monday, Tuesday, etc.
Dim c
'Set the column widths
   grdSched.ColWidth(0) = 600  'Column 0 is the time
   For c = 1 To 7              'Columns 1-7 are the day of week
     grdSched.ColWidth(c) = 1000
   Next c
'Put the days in the column headings, row 0
   grdSched.Row = 0           'Set the row to 0
   grdSched.Col = 1           'Set the column
   grdSched.Text = "Monday"
   grdSched.Col = 2
   grdSched.Text = "Tuesday"
   grdSched.Col = 3
```

```
      grdSched.Text = "Wednesday"
      grdSched.Col = 4
      grdSched.Text = "Thursday"
      grdSched.Col = 5
      grdSched.Text = "Friday"
      grdSched.Col = 6
      grdSched.Text = "Saturday"
      grdSched.Col = 7
      grdSched.Text = "Sunday"
End Sub

Sub rowHeading ()          'label rows 9AM, 10AM...11PM
Dim hr, AMPM
'Put the time in column 0, 9AM, 10AM, etc.
      grdSched.Col = 0        'Set the column to 0
      grdSched.Row = 0        'Set the row to 0
      For hr = 9 To 23        'Schedule is 9AM to 11PM
         grdSched.Row = grdSched.Row + 1     'change to next row
         If hr > 12 Then AMPM = hr - 12 & "PM" Else AMPM = hr & "AM"
         grdSched.Text = AMPM
      Next hr
End Sub

Sub cmdAdd_Click () 'Add the item to every selected cell
Dim r, c
   For r = grdSched.SelStartRow To grdSched.SelEndRow
      grdSched.Row = r
      For c = grdSched.SelStartCol To grdSched.SelEndCol
         grdSched.Col = c
         grdSched.Text = txtItem.Text
      Next c
   Next r
End Sub

Sub mnuExit_Click ()
   End
End Sub

Sub mnuHelp_Click ()
   MsgBox "Type the activity in the 'Item to Add' box, then ✎
   ✎ highlight the cells to insert it in and Press ADD.", 0, "Help"
End Sub

Sub mnuPrint_Click ()
'Prints exactly what you see on the form to default printer
 PrintForm
End Sub
```

④ **Save the file** as B:\schedule.frm, save the project as B:\schedule.mak

Experiment: To delete, the user must delete from the text box, then "add" the null string to the cell. Add a delete command (in the menu, or as a command button).

The "Schedule 2" Program

This schedule uses a nested for loop to break the hour into 15 minute segments. The method is the same as for the first Schedule. This program includes a delete command and prints.

① Build the form:

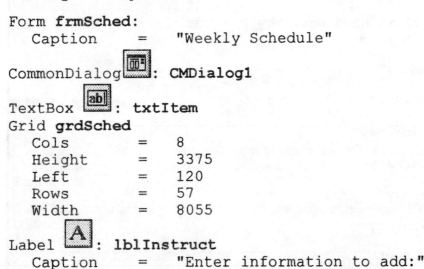

② Change the Properties:

```
Form frmSched:
   Caption    =    "Weekly Schedule"
```

CommonDialog 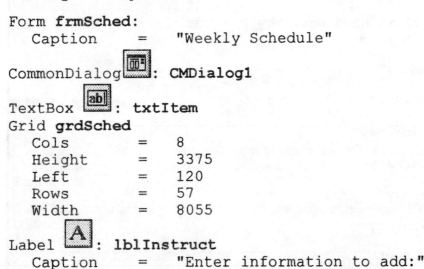: **CMDialog1**

TextBox : **txtItem**

Grid **grdSched**
```
   Cols      =    8
   Height    =    3375
   Left      =    120
   Rows      =    57
   Width     =    8055
```

Label : **lblInstruct**
```
   Caption    =    "Enter information to add:"
```

③ **Build the Menu:**

Caption	Name
&File	mnuFile
&Print	mnuPrint
-	mnuSep1
E&xit	mnuExit
&Add	mnuAdd
&Delete	mnuDelete

④ **Write the Code:** This is a long program. When you write a long program it is a good idea to write one or two procedures, then save, run, test, debug, save, then add the next procedure. For the code below, add the two general procedures without code, then each step can be tested, even if form_load calls a procedure with no code.

This program uses the string functions MID$ and Str$. See Appendix E for an explanation of the string functions.

```
Sub Form_Load ()
  columnHeadings
  rowHeadings
End Sub

Sub columnHeadings ()
Dim c
'Set the column widths
  grdSched.ColWidth(0) = 600
  For c = 1 To 7
    grdSched.ColWidth(c) = 1000
  Next c
'Put the days in the column headings, row 0
  grdSched.Row = 0
  grdSched.Col = 1
  grdSched.Text = "Monday"
  grdSched.Col = 2
  grdSched.Text = "Tuesday"
  grdSched.Col = 3
  grdSched.Text = "Wednesday"
  grdSched.Col = 4
  grdSched.Text = "Thursday"
  grdSched.Col = 5
  grdSched.Text = "Friday"
  grdSched.Col = 6
  grdSched.Text = "Saturday"
  grdSched.Col = 7
  grdSched.Text = "Sunday"
End Sub

Sub rowHeadings ()
 Dim hr, min, t
 Dim htext As String
 'Put the time in column 0, 9:00, 9:15, etc.
  grdSched.Col = 0
  grdSched.Row = 0
```

```
      For hr = 9 To 22
        If hr > 12 Then t = hr - 12 Else t = hr
        htext = Mid$(Str$(t), 2, 2) + ":"
        If t < 10 Then htext = " " + htext
        For min = 0 To 3
          grdSched.Row = grdSched.Row + 1
          If min = 0 Then
            grdSched.Text = htext + "00"
          Else
            grdSched.Text = htext + Mid$(Str$(min * 15), 2, 2)
          End If
        Next min
      Next hr
End Sub

Sub mnuExit_Click ()
  End
End Sub

Sub mnuAdd_Click ()
Dim r, c
  For r = grdSched.SelStartRow To grdSched.SelEndRow
    grdSched.Row = r
    For c = grdSched.SelStartCol To grdSched.SelEndCol
      grdSched.Col = c
      grdSched.Text = txtItem.Text
    Next c
  Next r
End Sub

Sub mnuDelete_Click ()
Dim r, c
  For r = grdSched.SelStartRow To grdSched.SelEndRow
    grdSched.Row = r
    For c = grdSched.SelStartCol To grdSched.SelEndCol
      grdSched.Col = c
      grdSched.Text = ""
    Next c
  Next r
End Sub

Sub mnuPrint_Click ()
Dim Row, Col
Dim Text As String
  On Error Resume Next
  CMDialog1.CancelError = True
  CMDialog1.Flags = &H100000  'Hide print to file
  CMDialog1.Action = 5        'printer
  printer.FontBold = True
  printer.Print "    WEEKLY SCHEDULE"
  printer.FontBold = False
  printer.Print  'blank line
  printer.FontUnderline = True
  For Row = 0 To 56 'Each column is 8 letters, shown 2 ways
    grdSched.Row = Row
    grdSched.Col = 0
```

```
'Exactly 8 letters are printed: take first 8, add if necessary
    Text = Left$(grdSched.Text & "         ", 8) & "|"
    printer.Print Text;
    For Col = 1 To 7
       grdSched.Col = Col
       Text = grdSched.Text & Space(8)    'Guarantee at least 8 letters
       Text = Left$(Text, 8) & "|"        'Guarantee exactly 8 letters
       printer.Print Text;
    Next Col
    printer.Print
    printer.FontUnderline = False
  Next Row
  printer.EndDoc
End Sub

Sub grdSched_SelChange()
'After selecting cells maybe they want to type an item?
  txtItem.SetFocus
End Sub
```

The Printed Report:

```
WEEKLY SCHEDULE
```

	Monday	Tuesday	Wednesda	Thursday	Friday	Saturday	Sunday
9:00	Coffee	Coffee	Coffee	Coffee	Coffee	Rest	Rest
9:15	Coffee	Coffee	Coffee	Coffee	Coffee	Rest	Rest
9:30	Coffee	Coffee	Coffee	Coffee	Coffee	Rest	Rest
10:00	Work	Work	Work	Work	Work	Rest	Rest
10:15	Work	Work	Work	Work	Work	Rest	Rest
10:30	Work	Work	Work	Work	Work	Rest	Rest
...							
10:45							

⑤ **Save the file** as B:\sched12.frm, **save the project** as B:\sched12.mak

Chapter 12

Adding Forms

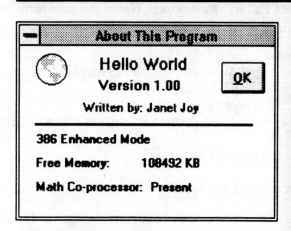

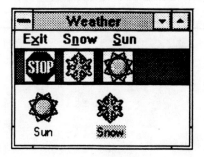

Add Forms at Design
Time

Create a Customized
Input Box

Create an "About Box"

Add Forms at
Run Time

Create an MDI
Application

Use DDE:
Dynamic Data
Exchange

Adding Forms at Design Time

The "Europe" Program illustrates adding forms to a project.

① **Change the name of Form1 to frmEurope** and build it as shown in the illustration:

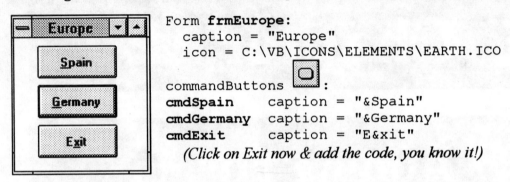

```
Form frmEurope:
    caption = "Europe"
    icon = C:\VB\ICONS\ELEMENTS\EARTH.ICO

commandButtons        :
cmdSpain      caption = "&Spain"
cmdGermany    caption = "&Germany"
cmdExit       caption = "E&xit"
```
(Click on Exit now & add the code, you know it!)

(Click on Exit now & add the code for cmdExit, you know it!)

② **Add form frmSpain**: From the menu select **File, New Form**. Name the new form frmSpain and build the form according to the illustration:

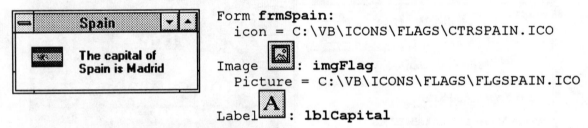

```
Form frmSpain:
    icon = C:\VB\ICONS\FLAGS\CTRSPAIN.ICO

Image       : imgFlag
    Picture = C:\VB\ICONS\FLAGS\FLGSPAIN.ICO

Label   : lblCapital
```

③ **Add form frmGermany** the same way you added frmSpain.

④ **Write the code for frmEurope:** The **<form>.show** command brings a form to the foreground.

```
Sub cmdSpain_Click ()
  frmSpain.Show
End Sub

Sub cmdGermany_Click ()
  frmGermany.Show
End Sub

Sub cmdExit_Click ()
  End
End Sub
```

Run the program. Click each command button and watch what happens to the forms. Try minimizing the forms. Notice the location of the forms.

Exercise: Delete the command buttons. Create a menu with the commands.
   Add other countries. Add the "Earth" icon to frmEurope with an Image Box.

⑤ **Save the forms** as europe.frm, germany.frm and spain.frm. Save the project as europe.mak.

Customized Input Boxes

Sometimes, you need a special input box or message box. You can design a message box or input box by adding a form. The "Day of Week" program uses a form to input the day of the week.

When the user clicks the command button, the form is shown as a modal form: it stays there until you make a selection. The day selected is then displayed on the start-up form.

① **Start a new project, and modify the form as shown below:**

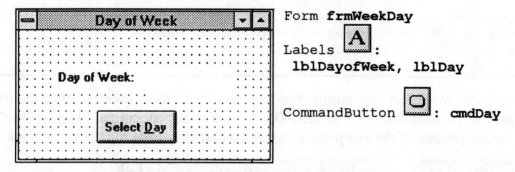

Form **frmWeekDay**

Labels [A] :
  lblDayofWeek, lblDay

CommandButton [▢] : **cmdDay**

② **Write the Code for frmWeekDay**

```
Sub cmdDay_Click ()
  frmSelectDay.Show 1
  If frmSelectDay.selection <> "" Then
    lblDay = frmSelectDay.selection
  End If
End Sub
```

Note: A form can access properties of another form; controls, and properties of the controls that are on the other form. A form can NOT access another forms variables. In order to access the day selected, a label is placed on the form. The day selected is placed in the label. In this example, the label is made invisible.

③ **Add a new form, frmSelectDay**: Select <u>F</u>ile, New <u>F</u>orm from the menu.

④ **Name the new form frmSelectDay and build as shown below:**

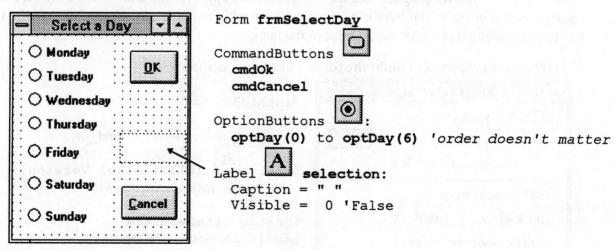

Form **frmSelectDay**

CommandButtons [▢]
    cmdOk
    cmdCancel

OptionButtons [◉] :
    optDay(0) to **optDay(6)** *'order doesn't matter*

Label [A] **selection**:
    Caption = " "
    Visible = 0 'False

⑤ **Write the Code for `frmSelectDay`:**

```
Sub cmdCancel_Click ()
  selection = "" 'Make the selection null when they select cancel
  frmSelectDay.Hide
End Sub

Sub cmdOk_Click () 'Hide the form
  Me.Hide  'Another way to hide form: me is frmDaySelect here
End Sub

Sub optDay_Click (index As Integer)
  'Copy the caption of the selected option to label
  selection = optDay(index).Caption
End Sub
```

When the user clicks the Select Day button, the "Select a Day" form appears. After the user selects Thursday and presses OK, the "Select a Day" form is hidden and the "Day of Week" form shows the day selected. If the user presses Cancel, no change is made to the Day of Week.

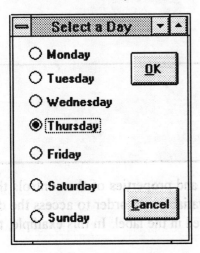

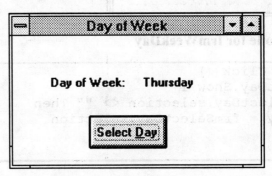

⑥ **Save the forms** as `weekday.frm` and `selctday.frm`
`Save the project as weekday.mak.`

Creating an "About" Box

Almost every Windows program has an "About" box. The "About Box" is shown here as a separate program. After you have it working, you can add the file to any project, change the title and save it under a new name. Add **About** to the menu.

① **Start a new project, and build the form** `frmAbout` **as shown:**

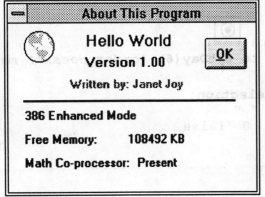

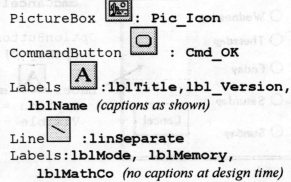

PictureBox ⬜ : `Pic_Icon`

CommandButton ⬜ : `Cmd_OK`

Labels ⬜ :`lblTitle,lbl_Version,`
`lblName` *(captions as shown)*

Line ⬜ :`linSeparate`
Labels:`lblMode, lblMemory,`
`lblMathCo` *(no captions at design time)*

② Change the Properties as shown below:

```
Form frmAbout
    BorderStyle      =    3   'Fixed Double
    Caption          =    "About This Program"
    ClipControls     =    0   'False
    MaxButton        =    0   'False
    MinButton        =    0   'False
PictureBox Pic_Icon
    AutoSize         =    -1  'True
    BorderStyle      =    0   'None
    Picture          select an icon
CommandButton Cmd_OK
    Caption        = "&OK"
Label lblName
    Caption        = "Written by: <your name>"
    ForeColor      = red
Line linSeparate
    BorderWidth    = 2
```

③ Write the code: This program calls external functions in a dynamic link library (DLL). Detailed explanation is not given, because it is unlikely that you would change the code. Search for "LIB" in help for another example.

```
Option Explicit
DefInt A-Z
Declare Function GetFreeSpace Lib "Kernel" (ByVal wFlags) As Long
Declare Function GetWinFlags Lib "Kernel" () As Long

Sub Cmd_OK_Click ()
  Unload frmAbout
End Sub

Sub Form_KeyPress (KeyAscii As Integer)
  Unload frmAbout
End Sub

Sub Form_Load ()
  Dim WinFlags As Long
  Dim Mode As String, processor As String
  WinFlags = GetWinFlags() 'Get current Windows configuration
  If WinFlags And &H20 Then ' Determine Enhanced or Standard Mode
    lblMode = "386 Enhanced Mode"
  Else
    lblMode = "Standard Mode"
  End If
  lblMemory = "Free Memory:         " ' Find amount of free memory
  lblMemory = lblMemory & Format$(GetFreeSpace(0) \ 1024) & " KB"
  If WinFlags And &H400 Then    'Look for Math Co-Processor
    lblMathCo = "Math Co-processor:  Present"
  Else
    lblMathCo = "Math Co-processor:  None"
  End If
End Sub
```

④ Save the program as about.frm and about.mak.

Adding New Forms at Run Time

There are two forms in this project: frmStart and frmColor. New copies of frmColor are created at run time. The user selects a QBColor with a scroll bar, then selects Go to create a new form. The new forms are on top of each other. You can drag them around to see them, or add code to put each one in a new position.

① **Start a new project**: Design the form and change the properties as shown below:

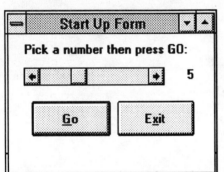

Form **frmStart** Caption= "Start Up Form"

Labels 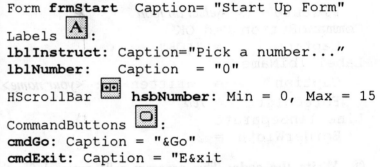:
lblInstruct: Caption="Pick a number..."
lblNumber: Caption = "0"

HScrollBar **hsbNumber**: Min = 0, Max = 15

CommandButtons:
cmdGo: Caption = "&Go"
cmdExit: Caption = "E&xit

② **Add a new form: frmColor**

CommandButton : **cmdOk**
   Caption = "&Ok"

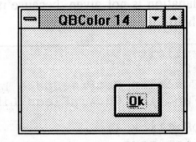

③ **Write the Code for frmStart:**

```
Sub cmdExit_Click ()
   End
End Sub

Sub cmdGo_Click ()
'Everytime we click GO, we get another COPY of frmColor.
Dim f As New frmColor
   f.Show
   f.BackColor = QBColor(frmStart.hsbNumber)
   f.Caption = "QBColor " & frmStart.hsbNumber
End Sub

Sub hsbNumber_Change ()
   lblNumber = hsbNumber
End Sub

Sub hsbNumber_Scroll ()
   lblNumber = hsbNumber
End Sub
```

④ **Write the Code for frmColor :**

```
Sub cmdOk_Click ()
   Me.Hide
End Sub
```

When you run the program, each of the color forms will be on top of each other: drag them around, try minimizing and clicking OK.

⑤ **Save** the forms as B:\start.frm and B:\color.frm.
Save the project as B:\clr_new.frm

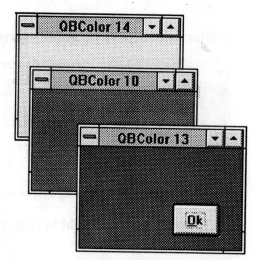

The modification below will cascade the forms as they are created:

```
Option Explicit
Dim lasttop, lastleft

Sub Form_Load ()
 lasttop = Top
 lastleft = Left + width
End Sub

Sub cmdGo_Click ()
Dim f As New frmColor
  f.Show
  f.BackColor = QBColor(frmStart.hsbNumber)
  f.Caption = "QBColor " & frmStart.hsbNumber
  lasttop = lasttop + 250
  f.Top = lasttop
  lastleft = lastleft + 250
  f.Left = lastleft
End Sub
```

MDI: Multiple Document Interface

When forms were shown in the "Europe" program, the forms could be displayed anywhere on the screen. When they were minimized, the icons could be anywhere on the screen. The "Weather" projects uses a multiple document interface (MDI). MDI Projects have one parent form, the MDI

form 📁. The other forms are called child forms 📄. Child forms (and their icons) will be contained within the MDI parent form. Even if the child forms are enlarged, they will still be contained within the parent form. The parent form will automatically get scroll bars if it needs them.

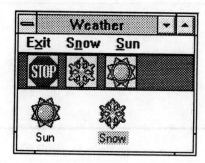

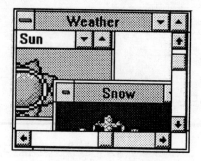

① Start a new project. Modify form1 as shown below:

```
Form frmSnow:
    Caption = "Snow"
    Icon = C:\VB\ELEMENTS\SNOW.ICO

Image  imgSnow:
    Picture = C:\VB\ELEMENTS\SNOW.ICO
    Stretch = -1  'True
```

Run the program. Minimize it, maximize it. When you get bored close it.

② Change the MDIChild property of the form to True.

Attempting to run the program now, produces and an error message:

③ Add an MDI Form: From the menu select
File, New MDI Form.
Name the MDI form **mdiWeather.**

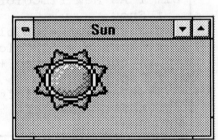

Run the program: the "Snow" program will be inside the MDI form.

④ Add another form. Name the new form **frmSun**.
It is exactly like the "Snow" form, except that it uses the
icon C:\VB\ELEMENTS\SNOW.ICO

Try running the program. Change the MDIChild property to true and run it again. When a child form is minimized, the icon is contained within the parent form. If a child form is closed, it is gone! In the next section, a menu is added to show the child forms again after they are closed and to make the sun appear.
(When you close the parent form, everything closes.)

⑤ Build a menu for mdiWeather:

Caption	Name
E&xit	mnuExit
S&now	mnuSnow
&Sun	mnuSun

⑥ Write the code for MDIForm:

```
Sub MDIForm_Load ()
  frmSnow.Show
  frmSun.Show
End Sub

Sub mnuExit_Click ()
  End        'End the entire application
End Sub
```

```
Sub mnuSnow_Click ()
  frmSnow.Show
End Sub

Sub mnusun_Click ()
  frmSun.Show
End Sub
```

⑦ Add a Tool Bar to the MDIForm:

You can't place anything directly on an MDI Form except a
control the has the "Align" property.
The picture box control has the align property.
Place a picture control on the MDIForm: name it picToolBar.
Draw three picture boxes inside the toolbar.

⑧ Change the properties according to the table:

```
PictureBox      picToolBar
    Align            =   1   'Align Top
    BackColor        select dark gray
PictureBox picStop drawn inside picToolBar
    BackColor        =   select light gray
    Picture          =   C:\VB\ICONS\TRAFFIC\TRFFC14.ICO
PictureBox picSnow drawn inside picToolBar
    BackColor        =   select light gray
    Picture          =   C:\VB\ICONS\ELEMENTS\SNOW.ICO
PictureBox picSun drawn inside picToolBar
    BackColor        =   select light gray
    Picture          =   C:\VB\ICONS\ELEMENTS\SUN.ICO
```

⑨ Write Code for the tool bar: *(The menu procedure contains the code: It is better to keep code in one place, in case you need to change it:*

```
Sub picSnow_Click ()
  mnuSnow_Click
End Sub

Sub picStop_Click ()
  mnuExit_Click
End Sub

Sub picSun_Click ()
  mnusun_Click
End Sub
```

Experiment: Add the following line:

```
  Sub MDIForm_Load ()
    frmSnow.Show
    frmRain.show
    Arrange 0
  End Sub
```

The Arrange statement arranges the forms or icons that are contained within the parent form:

Value	Meaning
0	Cascade all non-minimized MDI child forms.
1	Tile horizontal.
2	Tile Vertical.
3	Arrange Icons for minimized child forms.

The size of a form can be specified with the WindowState command. A value of 0 opens the form to its normal size; 1 opens it minimized (an icon); and 2 opens the window maximized:

Example: The code below will open the MDIForm with both of the child forms shown as icons.

```
Sub MDIForm_Load ()
  frmSnow.Show
  frmSnow.WindowState = 1
  frmSun.Show
  frmSun.WindowState = 1
End Sub
```

⑩ **Save** as `weather.frm`, `snow.frm`, and `sun.frm`. Save the project as `weather.mak`.

DDE: Dynamic Data Exchange

The "DDE" program combines the application to print a birthday card, and the application to print labels. The user can print a label, then use the name on the birthday card without having to retype the name.

The Label program will be the SOURCE program:

① **Open the LABEL.MAK project**: save the form as `DDE.FRM`, save the project as `DDE.MAK`

② **Change the properties**:
  frmLabel: **LINKMODE** property = **1** (*Source*).
  The name of the textbox where the name is typed <u>must</u> be **txtName**.

③ **Add the line shown below to Form_Load**: (LinkTopic could be something else, but it is important to use exact names in this exercise in order for the two **applications** to communicate with each other.)

```
Sub Form_Load ()
  grdLabel.Row = 0
  grdLabel.Col = 0
  frmLabel.LinkTopic = "Friend"
End Sub
```

④ **Run the program, save it, then create an EXE file called B:\DDE.EXE.**

The "Birthday" program will be the DESTINATION program:

⑤ **Load the BIRTHDAY.MAK project**: save the form as `HAPPY.FRM`, save the project as `HAPPY.MAK`.

⑥ **Modify the form:**
The name of the text box must be **txtFriend** for the code in this exercise to work.

Add a Command Button [□] : **cmdLink**

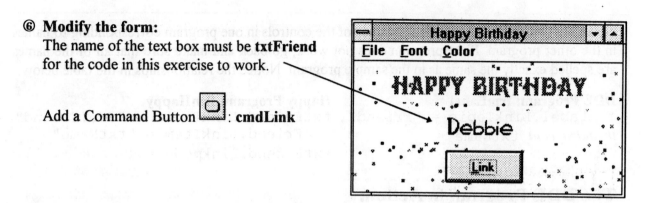

⑦**Add the following code for cmdLink** *(all other code is the same):*

```
Sub cmdLink_Click ()
  txtFriend.LinkTopic = "dde|Friend"
  txtFriend.LinkItem = "txtName"
  txtFriend.LinkMode = 1
End Sub
```

⑧ **Run the "Happy" program**: Type a name, print. If the Link button is pressed, an error message is generated because the DDE program is not running.

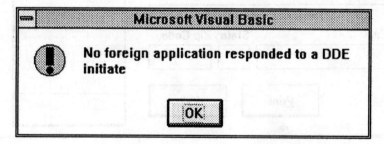

⑨ **Save the project and create an EXE file** called HAPPY.EXE, then *EXIT VISUAL BASIC!*

Run the applications: Execute file manager [▦] and start the "DDE" program and the "Happy" program: It will be easier to watch if everything else on the desktop is minimized.

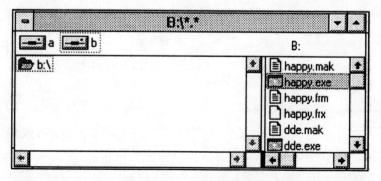

Type a name in the "DDE" (Label) program, then press Link in the "Happy" program: the name from the label program is immediately transferred to the "Happy" program. Try typing in each box, notice that the exchange is in one direction only. Names from the "Label" program get transferred to the "Happy" program but not the other way around.

Note: This program depends on the names of the controls in one program corresponding to names in the other program. If the program does not work, go back and make sure that all of the names are spelled exactly the same as in the sample program. Notice the relationships in the table below:

DDE Program: frmLabel

```
frmLabel.LinkTopic = "Friend"
```
the name is in `txtName`

Happy Program: frmHappy

```
txtFriend.LinkTopic = "dde|Friend"
txtFriend.LinkItem = "txtName"
txtFriend.Linkmode = 1
```

The DDE Program in Action:

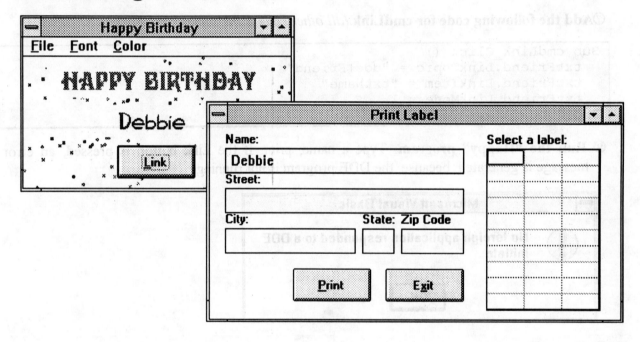

Chapter 13

Moving Things Around

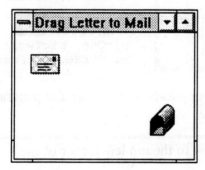

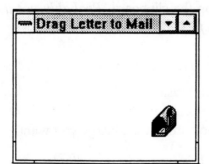

Use The Clipboard:

Add Copy, Cut & Paste to Applications

Use "Drag & Drop"

Write a "Matching Game"

The Clipboard

You have probably used the clipboard to copy text and pictures from one place to another. Anyone who is familiar with Windows expects to be able to use Ctrl+C to copy; Ctrl+X to cut, and Ctrl+V to paste. When a picture, or text is copied or cut, it is placed on the clipboard. Later, when the user issues the *paste* command, the contents of the clipboard are *pasted* into the selected area, replacing any selected text or graphic in that area. Cut is the same as copy, except that the original is erased. Once something is on the clipboard, it can be *pasted* as many times as desired.

The "Clipboard Program"

This program allows the user to Copy, Cut and Paste pictures and text within the application.

① **Build the form:**

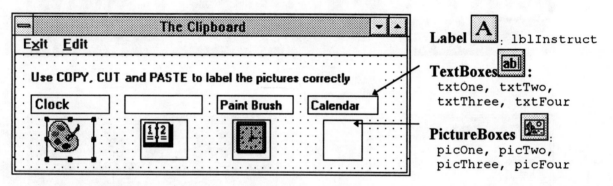

Label [A] : lblInstruct

TextBoxes [ab] :
txtOne, txtTwo,
txtThree, txtFour

PictureBoxes :
picOne, picTwo,
picThree, picFour

② **Add the pictures**: Any pictures could be used in the application. To write the program using the pictures shown in the example, follow the steps below:

❶ From program manager, move the **Accessories** window to the top left corner of the screen.

❷ Press Print Screen, this puts a picture of the screen on the clipboard. *Probably not the whole screen, that's why we moved Accessories to the top left.*

❸ Start Paintbrush

❹ Press Ctrl+V to paste the picture of the screen into Paintbrush.

❺ Click on the ✂ icon, then use the mouse to drag a box around the image you want.

❻ When the portion of the screen you want has a dotted line around it, press Ctrl+C
The selected image is now on the clipboard.

❼ Switch to Visual Basic, click the picture control where you want to paste the picture:
Press Ctrl+V to paste.

❽ Switch back and forth from Visual Basic and Paintbrush until you have copied all the pictures you need.

③ **Change Properties:** *change all captions as shown: captions labels do NOT match pictures!*
   frmEdit:
       Icon: *select* C:\VB\ICONS\WRITING\NOTE02.ICO

④ **Build the menu:**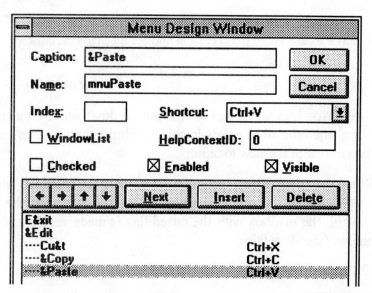

Caption	Name	Shortcut
E&xit	mnuExit	
&Edit	mnuEdit	
...Cu&t	mnuCut	Ctrl+X
...&Copy	mnuCopy	Ctrl+C
...&Paste	mnuPaste	Ctrl+V

Don't forget to select the Shortcut keys!

⑤ **Write The Code:** *The clipboard can contain either pictures or text. It is important to determine the type of control for any operation with the clipboard. Portions of the code below are similar, try using cut and paste to simplify the typing!*

```
Sub mnuCopy_Click ()'Method of copying depends on the active control
  Clipboard.Clear    'Erase anything in clipboard
  If TypeOf Screen.ActiveControl Is TextBox Then
    'text area of clipboard receives copy of selected text
    Clipboard.SetText Screen.ActiveControl.SelText
  ElseIf TypeOf Screen.ActiveControl Is PictureBox Then
    'data area of clipboard receives copy of picture in active control
    Clipboard.SetData Screen.ActiveControl.Picture
  End If
End Sub

Sub mnuCut_Click ()
  mnuCopy_Click   'Copy puts it on clipboard!
  'Cut erases:
  If TypeOf Screen.ActiveControl Is TextBox Then
    Screen.ActiveControl.SelText = ""    'No space between quotes!
  ElseIf TypeOf Screen.ActiveControl Is PictureBox Then
    'Erase picture by Load nothing
    Screen.ActiveControl.Picture = LoadPicture()
  End If
End Sub
```

```
Sub mnuExit_Click ()
  End   'End the program, clipboard retains anything placed in it!
End Sub

Sub mnuPaste_Click () 'Method of copying depends on active control
 If TypeOf Screen.ActiveControl Is TextBox Then
   'selected text is replaced by text from clipboard
   Screen.ActiveControl.SelText = Clipboard.GetText()
 ElseIf TypeOf Screen.ActiveControl Is PictureBox Then
   'picture in active control is replaced by picture from clipboard
   Screen.ActiveControl.Picture = Clipboard.GetData()
 End If
End Sub
```

⑥ **Save** as B:\clipbrd.frm and B:clipbrd.mak

Drag-Drop

Drag-Drop means to press the left mouse down while on a control; hold the left mouse down, and 'drag' the control to a new location with the mouse, then release the left mouse button to 'drop' the control in the new location.

When the "Drag-Drop" program starts, only the envelope and the empty mailbox are visible. The user can drag the envelope anywhere on the screen, if the envelope is dropped on the mailbox control, the mailbox with the raised flag is made visible and the envelope and empty mailbox are hidden (visible = false).

① **Build the Form:**

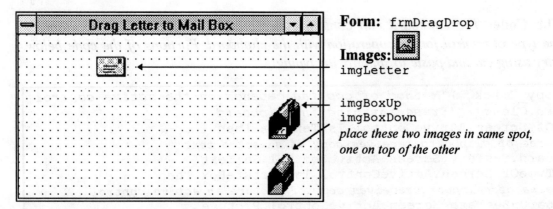

Form: frmDragDrop

Images:
imgLetter

imgBoxUp
imgBoxDown
place these two images in same spot,
one on top of the other

② **Change Properties:**

Image: imgBoxUp
      Picture = *select* C:\VB\ICONS\MAIL\MAIL16B.ICO
      Stretch = True
      Visible = False

Image imgBoxDown
      Picture = *select* C:\VB\ICONS\MAIL\MAIL16A.ICO
      Stretch = True
      Visible = True

Image imgLetter
    DragIcon = *select* C:\VB\ICONS\MAIL\MAIL03.ICO
    DragMode = Automatic
    Picture = *select* C:\VB\ICONS\MAIL\MAIL02A.ICO

③ **Write The Code:**

```
Option Explicit

Sub Form_DragDrop (Source As Control, X As Single, Y As Single)
 'moves the source object (letter image) to the position of mouse
 'Source will be the letter, X Y is position it is dropped
 Source.Move X, Y
End Sub

Sub imgBoxDown_DragDrop (Source As Control, X As Single,◊
  ◊ Y As Single)
  'Code is executed when a control (letter image) is dropped
  ' at the mailbox
  imgLetter.Visible = False     'hide the letter
  imgBoxDown.Visible = False    'hide the mailbox with flag down
  imgBoxUp.Visible = True       'show the mailbox with flag up
End Sub
```

④ **Save the file** as B:\dragdrop.frm, save the project as B:\dragdrop.mak

The Matching Game

This program uses Drag Drop to create a matching game to learn the flags of Europe. It save the high score as a text file.

① **Start a new project and build the form as shown below:**

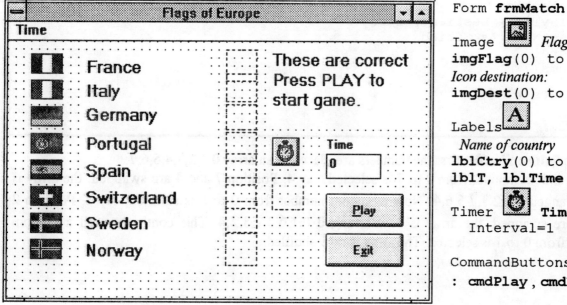

The flag of Italy icon is found in C:\VB\FLAGS\FLGITALY, there is also an icon that is an Italian flag shaped like a map of Italy called C:\VB\FLAGS\CTRITALY. The properties for imgFlag(1) are shown below. The other countries are done the same way. If there is no ctrFlag, the flgFlag is used as the drag icon.

② **Change the Properties:**

```
Label lblCtry(1)
   Caption      = "Italy"

Image imgObj(1)
   Picture      = C:\VB\FLAGS\FLGITALY
   DragIcon     = C:\VB\FLAGS\CTRITALY
   DragMode     = 1   'Automatic
```

Some controls are not labeled above:

```
Label lblInfo
   Caption      = "These are correct Press PLAY to start game."
```

Image **imgBlank** *(This is used for shuffling the icons)*

Image **imgDest**(0) to (7) *(When the user gets one right, the icon lands in these)*
```
   Left         = 3360
```

Label **lbltime**
```
   Caption               = "Time"
```

③ **The menu has a single item: mnuTime with the caption Time**

④ **The code is long. It is suggested that you write, save, and test in pieces.**

```
Option Explicit
Dim selection
Dim PlayTime, bestTime, ready
Dim bestName As String
Dim done
Dim nums(7)

Sub cmdExit_Click ()
 End
End Sub
```

The procedure Shuffle: first the numbers are placed in an array 0,1,2,3,4,5,6,7.
Next a random number from 0 to 7 is selected: say 4. Position 7 and 4 are swapped. the array is now arranged 0,1,2,3,**7**,5,6,**4**. Now a random number from 0 to 6 is selected, say 2. Position 2 and 6 are swapped: the array is now arranged 0,1,**6**,3,7,5,**2**,4. This continues until a random number from 0 to 1 is selected. The array is now shuffled.

```
Sub shuffle ()   'Shuffle the numbers in array NUM
Dim X, Y, temp
  For X = 0 To 7    'Put numbers in array in order
    nums(X) = X
  Next X
  For X = 7 To 1 Step -1
    Y = Int(X * Rnd)  'Swap position X and Y:
    temp = nums(Y)
    nums(Y) = nums(X)
    nums(X) = temp
  Next X
End Sub
```

Example: The table below shows the values in the array **nums** as successive random numbers Y are selected:

Nums		X=7 Y=4	X=6 Y=0	X=5 Y=2	X=4 Y=3	X=3 Y=0	X=2 Y=2	X=1 Y=0
0	0	0	**6**	6	6	**7**	7	**1**
1	1	1	1	1	1	1	1	**7**
2	2	2	2	**5**	5	5	**5**	5
3	3	3	3	3	**7**	**6**	6	6
4	4	**7**	**7**	7	**3**	3	3	3
5	5	5	5	**2**	2	2	2	2
6	6	6	**0**	0	0	0	0	0
7	7	**4**	4	4	4	4	4	4

The procedure shuffleNum uses the shuffled array to arrange the flags and countries:

```
Sub shuffleNum () 'Shuffle the flags and names of countries
Dim X, Y
shuffle
  For X = 0 To 7   'Shuffle the flags
    Y = nums(X)
    imgFlag(Y).Top = 100 + (X * 450)
    imgFlag(Y).Visible = True
  Next X
shuffle
  For X = 0 To 7    'Shuffle the country names
    Y = nums(X)
    imgDest(Y).Top = 200 + (X * 450)
    lblCtry(Y).Top = 200 + (X * 450)
    imgDest(Y).Picture = imgBlank.Picture
  Next X
End Sub

Sub Timer1_Timer () 'Ready is set to 1 when they push Play.
  If ready = 1 Then
    PlayTime = PlayTime + 1
    lblTime.Caption = PlayTime
  End If
End Sub
```

```
Sub cmdPlay_Click ()
 shuffleNum
 done = 0
 PlayTime = 0
 ready = 1
 lblInfo.Caption = "Drag the icon to the label"
End Sub
```

The procedure below keeps track of which flag is being dragged and dropped: The variable `selection` will be used to check if the flag selected is dropped on the correct label.

```
Sub imgFlag_MouseMove (Index As Integer, Button As Integer, ↺
 ↺ Shift As Integer, X As Single, Y As Single)
 selection = Index
End Sub
```

The user can drop the flag on the label or on the destination:

```
Sub imgDest_DragDrop (Index As Integer, Source As Control, ↺
 ↺ X As Single, Y As Single)
 If Index = selection Then
   correct
 Else
   lblInfo.Caption = "NO"
 End If
End Sub

Sub lblCtry_DragDrop (Index As Integer, Source As Control,
 ↺ X As Single, Y As Single)
 If Index = selection Then
   correct
 Else
   lblInfo.Caption = "NO"
 End If
End Sub
```

If they drop the flag in the right place, the flag is put into the destination slot. It is hidden on the left. The number of correct moves is counted. When they have done 8 correctly, the game is over.

```
Sub correct ()
  imgDest(selection).Picture = imgFlag(selection).Picture
  imgFlag(selection).Visible = False
  lblInfo.Caption = "Good"
  done = done + 1
  If done = 8 Then finished
End Sub
```

```
Sub finished ()
Dim message
  If PlayTime < bestTime Then
    newBestTime
  Else
    message = "Time = " + PlayTime
    MsgBox message, 0, "Game Over"
    'frmMsg.Hide
  End If
  cmdPlay.Visible = True
  ready = 0
End Sub
```

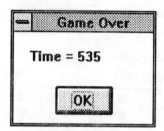

All of the procedures below involve reading and writing the Best time to a text file:

```
Sub getBestTime ()
  On Error Resume Next
  Open "match.dta" For Input As #1
  If Not EOF(1) Then Input #1, bestTime
  If Not EOF(1) Then Input #1, bestName
  Close
End Sub

Sub Form_Load ()
  Randomize
  bestTime = 3000   'Default in case no file exists
  PlayTime = 3000
  getBestTime
End Sub

Sub mnuTime_Click ()   'Look at the best time
  Dim message
  message = bestName & ": " & bestTime
  MsgBox message, 0, "Time"
End Sub
```

```
Sub newBestTime ()
  Dim message, title
  bestTime = PlayTime
  message = "New High Score: " & PlayTime
  message = message & Chr$(10) & Chr$(10)
  message = message & "Please enter your name:"
  bestName = InputBox(message, "Game Over", "")
  Open "match.dta" For Output As #1
  Print #1, bestTime, bestName
  Close
End Sub
```

⑤ **Save the file** as B:\match.frm, save the project as B:\match.mak

Exercise: Modify the program to match other items. Try matching a different number of items.

Chapter 14

The Data Control

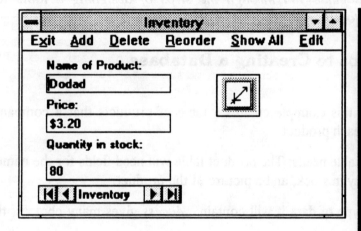

Learn What a Database is

Create an Access Database

Read, Write & Update the Database in Visual Basic

Use dBase

What Is A Database

A database is made up of one or more files (Microsoft Access calls them *Tables*). A file is made up of records. A record is made up of fields, or pieces of information.

Example: A company keeps information about salespeople. The salesperson *file* has one *record* for each salesperson. The record for each salesperson contains *fields* for name, social security number, and other *fields*.

If the files are "related" to each other through common keys, it is called a *relational* database.

Example: The company has a file of customers: one record for each customer. One of the fields in the customer record is the social security number of a salesperson (the customers "sales rep"). The customer file is *related* to the salesperson file through the salespersons social security number.

A database that contains only one table is called a "flat" database.

Each field in a database stores a certain type of data such as text, a date, or integers.
(*It is beyond the scope of this book to discuss all of the details of database design or database management. This exercise will guide you through the steps of designing a table to store information about product inventory.*)

Steps to Creating a Database

Design the Database on Paper:

① Decide on a table to create: this example creates a table of products that a company sells. There will be one record for each product.

② Determine the fields that the table needs: The product table will need fields for the name of the product, the price, the quantity in stock, and a picture of the product.

③ For each field, decide what type of data it will contain: *Access* gives many choices, the data types used in this table are:

Product Name: **Text** (For text fields, you must give the maximum length of the field.)

Example: State would be text with a length of 2.

Price: Currency

Quantity: **Integer**: used for whole numbers that will be used in arithmetic operations. If no arithmetic operations will be performed on the data, use text.

Example: a phone number would be text because we will not want to do any arithmetic operations on a phone number, such as finding the average phone number of all your friends.

Picture of Product: Memo

④ Decide on the key field, or index, the field that you would most likely use to look up information. For this example, the Product Name will be the index.

On The Computer

Creating an ACCESS database with DATAMGR.EXE

Visual Basic includes a program called `DATAMGR.EXE` that allows you to create an ACCESS database. (It does not have the full power of ACCESS). After creating a database, you can write a Visual Basic program to add, delete and update records in the database.

① From Windows Program Manager, select File Manger:

② From File Manager, change to the `C:\VB` sub-directory. Find `DATAMGR.EXE` and double click it.

③ From the `Data Manager` menu select:
`FILE, NEW DATABASE, ACCESS 1.1`

④ The file dialog window will allow you to select a drive and filename:
Name the file `B:INVENT.MDB`

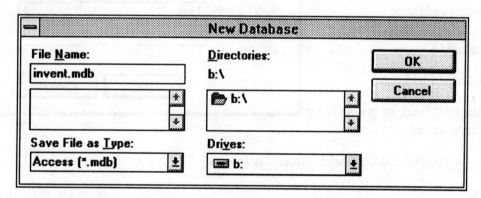

⑤ The Table Window will appear: select **New**

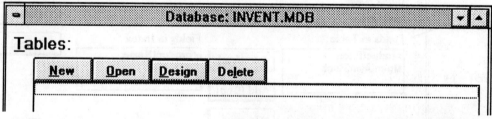

Name the table `Product`, then click OK.

⑥ When the table design window appears, select **Add** for each of the fields in the table below.

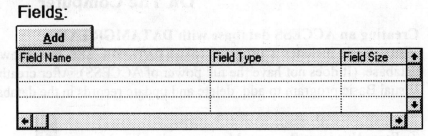

Field Name	Field type	Size
ProductName	Text	12
ProductPrice	Currency	
QuantityInStock	Integer	
ProductPicture	Memo	

For each field follow the steps below:

❶ Type the Field Name _____

❷ Press [Tab] to move to field type _____
Select a field type from the drop down list:
Do NOT type the field type.

❸ For text fields, enter the Field Size.

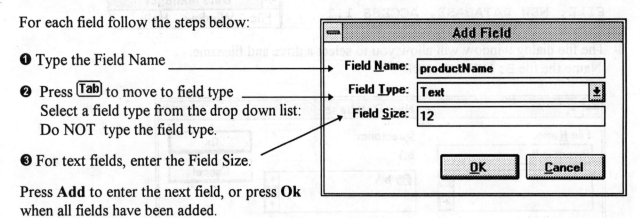

Press **Add** to enter the next field, or press **Ok** when all fields have been added.

⑦ Assign an INDEX for the table. Select **Add** under **Indexes**:

Select **ProductName** from the Fields in Table list.

Press **Add (Asc)**
   (ascending)

Type **Product as** Index name.

Check the two boxes at bottom.

Press **Done**.

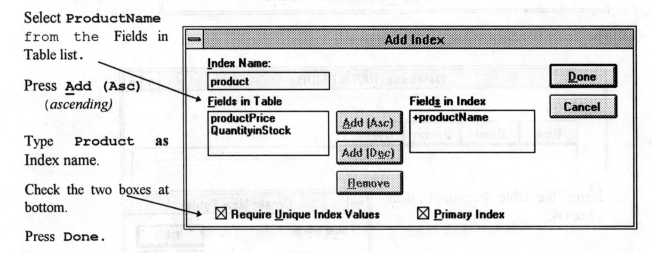

⑧ **Close the "Table: Product" window.**

Add Records to the Database: The database now has 1 table, Product, which is highlighted: Select **O**pen.

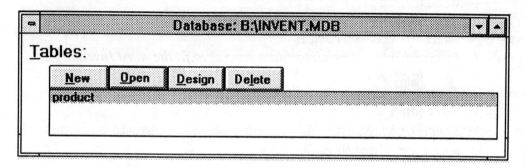

⑨ Select **A**dd for each record in the table. Enter each record by typing the information and pressing Tab to move to the next field. *(Do not enter anything for Memo)*

ProductName	ProductPrice	QuantityInStock
Widget	2.95	100
Gizmo	7.50	0
Doodad	3.20	75
Thingamabob	1.40	0
Dohickey	4.00	80
Geegaw	1.99	217

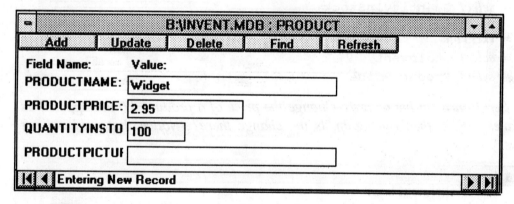

Click ⊟ after adding all of the products.

⑩ **Exit DATA MANAGER.** The ACCESS database has been created. The next step is to write a Visual Basic program to use it.

A Visual Basic Interface for the DataBase

Start Visual Basic

① **Start a new project.** Name the form `frmInvent` and save the file as `B:INVENT.FRM`; save the project as `INVENT.MAK`.

② Place the data control on the form ▦. Change the following properties:

```
Name          = dtaInvent
Caption       = "Inventory"
DatabaseName  = select B:\INVENT.MDB
RecordSource  = "product"   (Stretch the data control to fit the word Inventory.)
```

③ Place a text box on the form [abl]. Change the following properties:

```
Name        = txtProduct
DataSource  = select dtaInvent
DataField   = select productName
```

Run the program: Use the data control to look at the products:

|◄◄ ◄   ► ►|

First, Previous, Next, Last

④ Add a text box [abl] **for each field (except memo).** Change the properties as shown:

```
Name        = txtQuantity
DataSource  = select dtaInvent
DataField   = select QuantityInStock


Name        = txtPrice
DataSource  = select dtaInvent
DataField   = select ProductPrice
```

Run the program. Scroll through the records. Change the price of a product. What happens? Is the change permanent? Exit, then run again, is the change there? (Notice that we have not written any code yet!)

⑤ Place a label [A] **over each text box:**

```
Name     = lblProduct
Caption  = "Product:"
Name     = lblPrice
Caption  = "Price:"
Name     = lblQuantity
Caption  = "Quantity:"
```

Does it irritate you that some of the prices have only one place after the decimal?

⑥ Add the following code:

```
Sub txtPrice_Change ()
  txtPrice = Format(txtPrice, "$##0.00")
End Sub
```

When this project is finished, we will be able to exit; add records; delete records; view only those products that need to be ordered, and use the edit commands - copy, cut and paste.

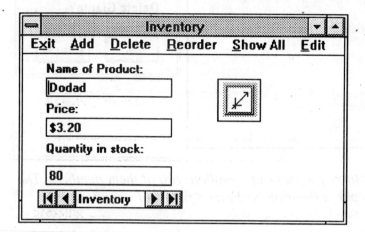

⑦ **Build the Menu:**

Caption	Name	Shortcut Key
E&xit	mnuExit	
&Add	mnuAdd	
&Delete	mnuDelete	
&Reorder	mnuReorder	
&Show All	mnuAll	
&Edit	mnuEdit	
Cu&t	mnuCut	Ctrl+X
&Copy	mnuCopy	Ctrl+C
&Paste	mnuPaste	Ctrl+V

⑧ **Add Code:** This is a long program, add the procedures, save and test as you go along:

```
Sub mnuExit_Click ()   'Close the database and exit:
  dtaInvent.Recordset.Close
  End
End Sub

Sub mnuReorder_Click ()
  'View only the products that need to be reordered
  dtaInvent.RecordSource = "Select * from Product where ↺
    ↺ QuantityinStock < 20"
  dtaInvent.Refresh
End Sub

Sub mnuAll_Click ()   'View all of the products again
  dtaInvent.RecordSource = "Select * from Product"
  dtaInvent.Refresh
End Sub
```

```
Sub mnuDelete_Click ()
'Delete a record - Confirm the delete first:
Dim msg, ans
  msg = "Delete "
  msg = msg & dtaInvent.Recordset("ProductName")
  msg = msg & "?"
  ans = MsgBox(msg, 1, "Delete Record")
  If ans = 1 Then
     dtaInvent.Recordset.Delete
     dtaInvent.Recordset.MoveNext
  End If
End Sub
```

When we add a record, we have to ask for three pieces of information: two of them numbers. The function getNumber receives two words to put in the prompt: Enter <field> of <product>.

GetNumber loops until a valid number is entered or cancel is pressed. It returns -1 if the user presses cancel:

```
Function getNumber (field, product)
 Dim msg, number
 msg = "Enter " & field & " of " & product
 Do
    number = InputBox(msg, "Enter Number")
    If number = "" Then number = -1
    If Not IsNumeric(number) Then
       msg = "Not a valid number: Enter " & field & " of " & product
    End If
 Loop Until IsNumeric(number)
 getNumber = number  'return number to calling procedure
End Function
```

The procedure mnuAdd will stop asking for information as soon as the user presses cancel. The program will crash if we try to add a name that is bigger than the size of product name. The function Left$ and the size of product name are used to extract the right number of letters from the name the user entered:

```
Sub mnuAdd_Click ()
Dim nameSize, product, price, quantity
nameSize = dtaInvent.Recordset("ProductName").Size
dtaInvent.Recordset.AddNew
product = InputBox("Product Name:", "Add Product")
 If product <> "" Then
   product = Left$(product, nameSize)
   price = getNumber("Price", product)
   If price <> -1 Then
    quantity = getNumber("Quantity", product)
    If quantity <> -1 Then
     dtaInvent.Recordset("ProductName") = product
     dtaInvent.Recordset("ProductPrice") = price
     dtaInvent.Recordset("QuantityinStock") = quantity
```

```
      dtaInvent.Recordset.Update
    End If 'did not cancel on quantity
  End If 'did not cancel on price
 End If 'did not cancel on product name
End Sub
```

The last step in this project is to add a picture of the product:

⑨ **Place a picture box** [icon] **on the form and change the properties:**

```
Name          =  picProduct
AutoSize      =  True
DataSource    =  "dtaInvent"
DataField     =  "productPicture"
```

To add a picture to the database, the user must select Switch To, then use the Paintbrush program to draw a picture, or select it from a file. The user then clicks on the picture control and uses [Ctrl]+V to paste the picture. The pasted picture becomes part of the database. The same edit command that were written earlier are used here: *(Maybe they should go into a module!)*

Add the code for the edit commands:

```
Sub mnuCopy_Click ()
 Clipboard.Clear
 If TypeOf Screen.ActiveControl Is TextBox Then
    Clipboard.SetText Screen.ActiveControl.SelText
 ElseIf TypeOf Screen.ActiveControl Is PictureBox Then
    Clipboard.SetData Screen.ActiveControl.Picture
 End If
End Sub

Sub mnuCut_Click ()
 mnuCopy_Click
 If TypeOf Screen.ActiveControl Is TextBox Then
    Screen.ActiveControl.SelText = ""
 ElseIf TypeOf Screen.ActiveControl Is PictureBox Then
    Screen.ActiveControl.Picture = LoadPicture()
 End If
End Sub

Sub mnuPaste_Click ()
 If TypeOf Screen.ActiveControl Is TextBox Then
    Screen.ActiveControl.SelText = Clipboard.GetText()
 ElseIf TypeOf Screen.ActiveControl Is PictureBox Then
    Screen.ActiveControl.Picture = Clipboard.GetData()
 End If
End Sub
```

⑩ **Save the file** as B:\invent.frm, save the project as B:\invent.mak

Other Databases

Visual Basic has a file called **C:\VB\EXTERNAL.TXT**, this file gives complete information for accessing other databases such as Paradox, Fox Pro, and others. The file also contains some lines that must be inserted into the **C:\WINDOWS\VB.INI** before Visual Basic can use the other database. This file also gives some advice on updating and accessing the external files. The steps below on accessing dBase IV are similar for other external databases. The file **C:\VB\EXTERNAL.TXT** has information on several other databases. If you are using an external database (not Access) this file contains the information you will need.

Accessing a dBASE IV Database from Visual Basic

Visual Basic allows you to create and access "Access" databases with very little work. Visual Basic also allows you to access (but not create) other database files. Suppose you have a dBase IV file, called **B:\EMPLOY.DBF** that you would like to access.

The **C:\WINDOWS\VB.INI** needs a section to setup external databases. If this section is missing, you will get the error "Cannot find installable ISAM."

The file **C:\VB\EXTERNAL.TXT** has lots of useful information about external files, including the necessary lines for the **VB.INI** file.

① Open the **C:\VB\EXTERNAL.TXT** file in notebook and COPY, [Ctrl]+**C** the lines below:

```
[Installable ISAMs]
dBASE III=C:\WINDOWS\SYSTEM\xbs110.dll
dBASE IV=C:\WINDOWS\SYSTEM\xbs110.dll
[dBase ISAM]
Deleted=On
PageTimeout=5          ;500 ms-non-read-locked page timeout
MaxBufferSize=128  ;128K
LockRetry=20           ;20 - retries on Read/Write locks
CommitLockRetry=20 ;20 - retries on Commit locks
ReadAheadPages=16  ;16 pages
```

② Open **C:\WINDOWS\VB.INI** in notebook and paste [Ctrl]+**V** the lines at the end of file.

③ Place the data control on the form. Name the data control dtaEmployee.

Set the following properties of the data control (data1):

Connect	**dBase IV**	*Specify database type*
DatabaseName	**B:**	*Path only of database file*
RecordSource	**EMPLOY**	*Name of database table file*

④ Everything else works just like an Access database. Add text boxes for each field, and add the code. You do not need to know the names, just select from the drop-down list.

Appendix A: ANSI Character Set

Characters are available using CHR(*number*), or entered from the keyboard using [Alt]+*number*.

008	*backspace*	067	C	106	j	178	²	217	Ù
009	*tab*	068	D	107	k	179	³	218	Ú
010	*linefeed*	069	E	108	l	180	´	219	Û
013	*return*	070	F	109	m	181	µ	220	Ü
032	*space*	071	G	110	n	182	¶	221	Ý
033	!	072	H	111	o	183	·	222	Þ
034	"	073	I	112	p	184	¸	223	ß
035	#	074	J	113	q	185	¹	224	à
036	$	075	K	114	r	186	º	225	á
037	%	076	L	115	s	187	»	226	â
038	&	077	M	116	t	188	¼	227	ã
039	'	078	N	117	u	189	½	228	ä
040	(	079	O	118	v	190	¾	229	å
041	)	080	P	119	w	191	¿	230	æ
042	*	081	Q	120	x	192	À	231	ç
043	+	082	R	121	y	193	Á	232	è
044	,	083	S	122	z	194	Â	233	é
045	-	084	T	123	{	195	Ã	234	ê
046	.	085	U	124	|	196	Ä	235	ë
047	/	086	V	125	}	197	Å	236	ì
048	0	087	W	126	~	198	Æ	237	í
049	1	088	X	160	*space*	199	Ç	238	î
050	2	089	Y	161	¡	200	È	239	ï
051	3	090	Z	162	¢	201	É	240	ð
052	4	091	[	163	£	202	Ê	241	ñ
053	5	092	\	164	¤	203	Ë	242	ò
054	6	093	]	165	¥	204	Ì	243	ó
055	7	094	^	166	¦	205	Í	244	ô
056	8	095	_	167	§	206	Î	245	õ
057	9	096	`	168	¨	207	Ï	246	ö
058	:	097	a	169	©	208	Ð	247	÷
059	;	098	b	170	ª	209	Ñ	248	ø
060	<	099	c	171	«	210	Ò	249	ù
061	=	100	d	172	¬	211	Ó	250	ú
062	>	101	e	173	-	212	Ô	251	û
063	?	102	f	174	®	213	Õ	252	ü
064	@	103	g	175	¯	214	Ö	253	ý
065	A	104	h	176	°	215	×	254	þ
066	B	105	i	177	±	216	Ø	255	ÿ

Appendix B: Controls

Name	Icon	Prefix	Use	Properties
Check box		chk	Any number of check boxes can be checked at one time	DataField, DataSource
Combo box		cbo	Allows user to select from a drop down list	Sorted
Command button		cmd	User selects it to execute a command	Font*, color*, Enabled, Cancel
Common Dialog			Allows common dialog boxes for color, font, and file operations at run time	
Data		dta	Connects to database to display information from database	DataBaseName, Exclusive, RecordSource
Directory list box		dir	Allows selection of directories and sub-directories	Font*, Color*
Drive list box		drv	allows selection of valid drive	Font*, Color*
File list box		fil	Allows selection from a list of files using a pattern such as *.DTA	Archive, Pattern (*.*) ReadOnly, system
Form		frm	The visible run time window	Controlbox, Icon, Picture, MDIchild
Frame		fra	Provides grouping of controls	ClipControls, Font*
Grid		grd	Allows organization of data in rows and columns	FillStyle, Cols, Rows, GridLines, GridLineWidth
Horizontal scroll bar		hsb	Allows selection of a value from a range	Max, Min, SmallChange, MousePointer
Image		img	For display of *.BMP, *.ICO and *.WMF files	Picture, Stretch
Label		lbl	Display only; user cannot type in this box.	Alignment, WordWrap,
Line		lin	For drawing a straight line	DrawMode, X1, X2, Y1, Y2
List box		lst	Display a list of items to select from	Columns, MultiSelect, Sorted
OLE		ole	Object linking & embedding	*Link a wordart, paint, or graph application to your program.*
Option button		opt	Only one of options in a group or frame can be selected at once	Enabled, visible, value
Picture box		pic	For display of *.BMP, *.ICO and *.WMF files or a text area	ClipControls, DrawStyle, DrawWidth, fillColor, fillStyle, Align
Shape		shp	Add rectangle, square, oval, etc.	shape, color, fillstyle
Text box		txt	For input or display of text	DataField, DataSource, MultiLine, Scrollbars
Timer		tmr	Specify time intervals for events to occur	Interval
Vertical scroll bar		vsb	Allows selection of a value from a range	Max, Min, SmallChange, MousePointer

* Font and Color: Font* includes the properties fontSize, fontName, fontItalic, etc. Color* includes backColor and ForeColor.

Appendix C: Drawing Procedures

Line: The Line Procedure has this format: (*color and box are optional*)
```
Line (<x1>,<y1>)-(<x2>,<y2>),<color>,<box>
```

x1,y1 is the starting point of the line

x2,y2 is the end point of the line

color is optional, you can use either QBColor or RGB function.
```
Line(3,19)-(23,100),QBColor(5)
```

box is optional: if you want to draw a box instead of a line, put a **B** here
```
Line(0,0)-(12,60),QBColor(4),B
```

boxFilled: if you want the box to be filled in (solid), use **BF**
```
Line(5,5)-(14,50),QBColor(12),BF
```
If you want to specify Box, but no color use a comma
```
Line(5,3)-(30,20), ,B
```

Pset: The Pset procedure draws a single dot, the format is:
```
PSet(<x>,<y>),<color>
```

x and **y** are the coordinates of the points.

color is optional, you can use either QBColor or RGB function
```
PSet(5,20),RGB(255,0,0)
```

Circle: The Circle Procedure has this format:
```
Circle(<x>,<y>),<radius>,<color>,<start>,<end>,<aspect>
```

x and y are the coordinates of the center of the circle

radius is the radius based on the *scaleMode* property of the form.

color is optional, you can use either QBColor or RGB function.
```
circle(x,y),20,QBColor(4)
```

Start, end and aspect are used to draw, arcs, ellipses, etc. A full description of this method is in HELP! - if you're into circles, look it up in help and have fun!)

Examples make it clearer:

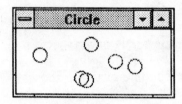 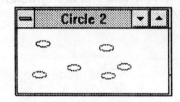 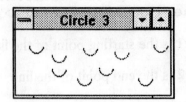

Circle uses only the x,y, radius and color arguments:
```
Circle(x,y),100,QBColor(5)
```

Circle 2 uses the *aspect* argument:
```
Circle(x,y),100,QBColor(5), , , .5
```

Circle 3 uses the *start* and *end* arguments:
```
Circle(x,y),100,QBColor(5),1*pi,2*pi
```

```
Option Explicit
Dim pi As Single 'needed because start and end must be in radians

Sub Form_Load ()
  pi = 3.14
End Sub

Sub Form_MouseDown (Button As Integer, Shift As Integer, ♦
   ♦x As Single, y As Single)
   Circle (x, y), 100, QBColor(5), 1 * pi, 2 * pi
End Sub
```

Appendix D: Using the File Dialog Window

The File Dialog Window opens when you click ⬛ : to open a file, or select an icon or picture.

The illustrations below show the steps to select the file named `C:\VB\ELEMENTS\EARTH.ICO`

The file dialog window opens with the current drive and directory selected. The example shows the B: drive selected:

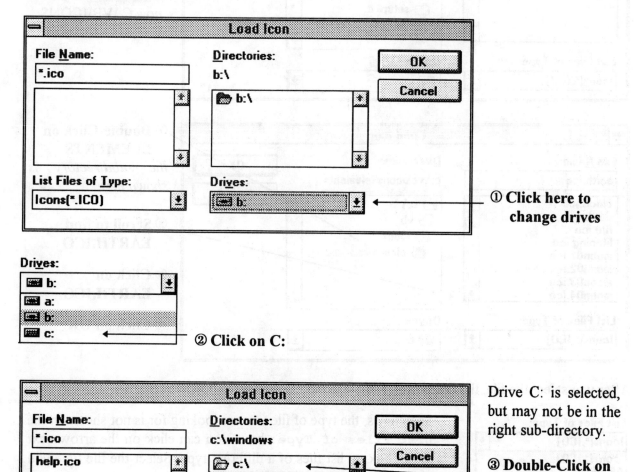

The sub-directories on your computer will probably be different.

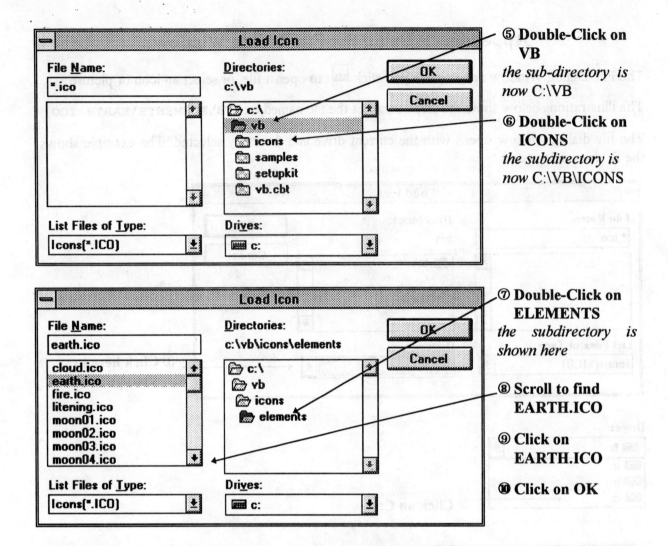

⑤ **Double-Click on VB**
the sub-directory is now C:\VB

⑥ **Double-Click on ICONS**
the subdirectory is now C:\VB\ICONS

⑦ **Double-Click on ELEMENTS**
the subdirectory is shown here

⑧ **Scroll to find EARTH.ICO**

⑨ **Click on EARTH.ICO**

⑩ **Click on OK**

After you select the file, the OK button will close the file dialog window.

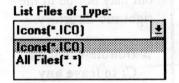

Sometimes, the type of file you are looking for is not shown in the `List Files of Type:` box. You can click on the arrow next to this box, to list files of a different type. Select the file type you are looking for by double-clicking.

Saving a file uses the same steps to select drive and directory, then you type the name here:

Appendix E: Built In Functions

Math Functions:

Abs(n) returns the absolute value of the n:
    caption = Abs(3) displays 3 in the caption;
    caption = Abs(-3) displays 3 in the caption;

Exp(n) Returns e^n (e is approximately 2.718282)

Fix(n) returns the integer portion of n
    caption = Fix(3.2) displays 3 in the caption
    caption = Fix(-3.2) displays -3

Int(n) returns the integer portion of n if n is positive, the next smaller integer if n is negative
    caption = Int(3.2) displays 3 in the caption
    caption = Int(-3.2) displays -4 in the caption

Log(n) Returns the natural logarithm of a number. N must be greater than 0.
    The natural logarithm is the logarithm to the base e.
    The constant e is approximately 2.718282.

Rnd Returns a random number $0 <= n < 1$.

Sgn(n) returns the sign of n
    If n > 0, then Sgn(n) returns 1.
    If n = 0, then Sgn(n) returns 0.
    If n < 0, then Sgn(n) returns -1.

Sqr(n) returns the square root of n: n must be >= 0

Angle Functions: Use the equations below for the angle functions:
    pi =3.141593
    Angles must be in radians:
        To convert degrees to radians: degrees = radians * 180/pi
        To convert radians to degrees: radians = degrees * pi / 180

Atn(n) Returns the arctangent in radians: n = side opposite angle/ side adjacent to the angle

Cos(<angle in radians>) Returns the cosine of an angle.

Sin(<angle in radians>) Returns the sine of an angle

Tan(<angle in radians>) Returns the tangent of an angle.

String Functions: All of the functions shown with a dollar sign return a string. The same value is returned as a variant type if you leave off the dollar sign.

Asc: `Asc(<character>)` returns the ASCII code for the character.
`caption = Asc("A")` displays **65** in the caption.

Chr$: `Chr$(<ASCII value>)` returns the character for the ASCII code.
`caption = Chr$(65)` displays **A** in the caption.

Left$: `Left$(<string>,<n>)` returns the leftmost n character of the string.
`caption = Left$("ABCDEFGHIJKL", 5)` displays **ABCDE** in the caption.

Mid$: `Mid$(<string>,<start>,<n>)` returns n characters beginning with start.
`caption = Mid$("ABCDEFGHIJKL", 3, 5)` displays **CDEFG** in the caption.

Len: `Len(<string>)` returns the number of letters in a string, including punctuation and spaces.
`caption = Len("Hello Out There!")` displays **16** in the caption.

Right$: `Right$(<string>,<n>)` returns the rightmost n characters of the string.
`caption = Right$("ABCDEFGHIJKL", 5)` displays **HIJKL** in the caption.

Space$: `Space(<number>)` returns a strings of number spaces.
`caption = "*" & Space(5) & "*"` displays ***   *** in the caption.

String$: `String (<n>,<string>)` returns a string repeating the first character in string n times.
`caption = String(10, "*")` displays ************** in the caption.
`caption = String(5, "ABC")` displays **AAAAA** in the caption.

String$: `String (<number>,<character code>)` returns a string repeating the character n times.
`caption = String(10, 42)` displays ************** in the caption.

Val: `Val(<string>)` converts a string to a number. It stops looking as soon as it comes to a character that can not be converted to a number.
`caption = Val("123 Main St.")` displays **123** in the caption.
`caption = Val("Extension 45")` displays **0** in the caption.

Date and Time Functions:

Now: returns the current system date and time as a double precision number, the date is to the left of the decimal, the time is to the right of the decimal. Now is usually used with a function to return the specific portion you are interested in:

Day(Now)   returns an integer from 1 to 31.

Month(Now)   returns an integer from 1 to 12.

Year(Now)   returns the 4 digit year.

Weekday(Now) returns an integer from 1 (Sunday) to 7 (Saturday).

Second(Now)   returns an integer from 0 to 59.

Minute(Now)   returns an integer from 0 to 59.

Hour(Now)   returns an integer from 0 to 23 (a 24 hour clock: 20 is 8 PM).

DATE$ returns a 10 character string of the format *mm-dd-yyyy*.

TIME$ returns an 8 character string of the format *hh:mm:ss*.

TIMER returns the seconds elapsed since 12:00AM (midnight) Timer is used in games:

```
start = timer
...play game...
finish = Timer
score = finish - start
```

Appendix F: QBColors

Some monitors may display slightly different colors:

Value	Color
0	Black
1	Blue
2	Green
3	Cyan
4	Red
5	Magenta
6	Yellow
7	White

Value	Color
8	Gray
9	Light Blue
10	Light Green
11	Light Cyan
12	Light Red
13	Light Magenta
14	Light Yellow
15	Bright White

Appendix G: Operator Precedence

Evaluate an expression in the following order:
1. Anything inside parenthesis, including functions, are done first: working from the inner-most parenthesis out;
2. Raise to a power: ^ is performed from left to right ;
3. Multiplication and division (*, /) are performed from left to right;
4. Mod is performed from left to right;
5. Addition and subtraction (+ and -) are performed from left to right.

Appendix H: Types Supported by Visual Basic

Data type	Suffix	Storage size	Range
Integer	%	2 bytes	-32,768 to 32,767
Long *(long integer)*	&	4 bytes	-2,147,483,648 to 2,147,483,647
Single *(single-precision floating-point)*	!	4 bytes	-3.402823E38 to -1.401298E-45 *negative* 1.401298E-45 to 3.402823E38 *positive*
Double *(double-precision floating-point)*	#	8 bytes	-1.79769313486232E308 to -4.94065645841247E-324 *negative* 4.94065645841247E-324 to 1.79769313486232E308 *positive*
Currency *(scaled integer)*	@	8 bytes	-922,337,203,685,477.5808 to 922,337,203,685,477.5807
String	$	1 byte per character	0 to approx. 65,500 bytes. *(Some storage overhead is required.)*
Variant	*none*	*varies*	*Any numeric value up to the range of a Double or any character text*
User-defined	*(using Type)*		*Number required by elements*

Appendix I: Message Boxes

There are six basic combinations of buttons:

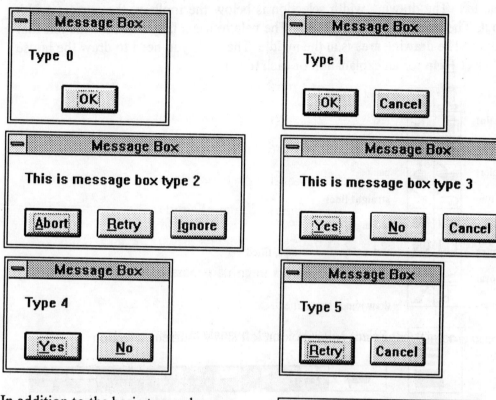

In addition to the basic types above, an
icon can be displayed as shown on the
right by adding one of four values (16, 32,
48 or 64) to the basic type.

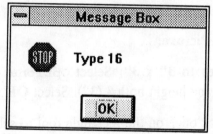

Add 16 to display the Stop Sign. **STOP**   Add 32 to display the Question mark. **?**

Add 48 to display the Exclamation point. **!**   Add 64 to display the letter I (information): **i**

Return Values: The buttons return the values in table below:

Button	Value
Ok	1
Cancel	2
Abort	3
Retry	4
Ignore	5
Yes	6
No	7

Appendix J: The Paint Program

When you start the Paint Program, you will see the following windows:
The toolbox is on the left. The drawing width selection is below the toolbox, the current width has an arrow next to it. The palette is on the bottom. The palette has a larger box on the left that shows the selected color. The drawing area is in the middle. The tools you need to draw the house are shown in bold. (Select **Help** for an explanation of each tool.)

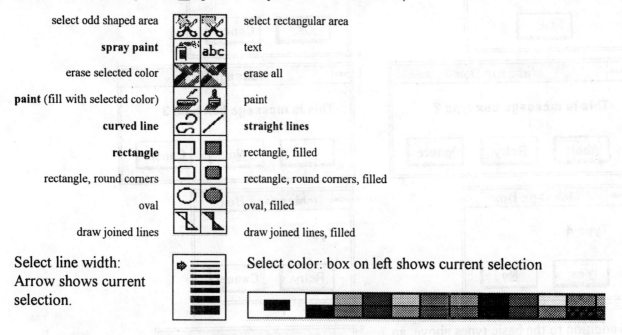

select odd shaped area · select rectangular area
spray paint · text
erase selected color · erase all
paint (fill with selected color) · paint
curved line · **straight lines**
rectangle · rectangle, filled
rectangle, round corners · rectangle, round corners, filled
oval · oval, filled
draw joined lines · draw joined lines, filled

Select line width:
Arrow shows current selection.

Select color: box on left shows current selection

To Create the House Picture:

Set the Drawing Area to 3" x 3": Select `Options, Image Attributes...,` select `in` (inch) make the width and height both 3 (3"). Select **OK**.

Draw the House: Click once on the rectangle tool to select it. Move the mouse to one corner of the house and press down on the left mouse button. Drag the mouse to the opposite corner of the house and release to draw a rectangle. Repeat to draw the windows and doors.

Draw the Roof & Chimney: You need lines for the roof, and the chimney. Select the line tool. Move the mouse pointer to the end point of one of the lines you need. Press down on the left mouse button, and drag the line to the length you want. Repeat to draw all five lines.

Paint the Door Red: Select red from the palette. Click on the paint roller to select it, then click once in the middle of the door. Paint the chimney, house and windows any color you like. If you make a mistake, select `Edit, Undo.` *(It undoes everything since you last selected a tool or color.)*

The Tree: Select green from the palette. Select the spray paint tool. Use the mouse button like you were holding a can of spray paint to paint the leaves. Use several shades of green and yellow. The Trunk: select the curved line tool. Drag a line, then click along the side of the trunk to make the line stretch and curve. The "spray paint" is also used for the smoke.

Edit: You can move parts of the drawing: first outline the area with one of the scissors tools. You can then move the selected area by *dragging*, or by using the copy [Ctrl]+C , cut [Ctrl]+X and paste [Ctrl]+V functions.

Save the File: Select <u>F</u>ile, <u>S</u>ave, name it B:\HOUSE.BMP

Appendix K: Using Setup Wizard to Create a Distribution Disk

You will need a disk with your Visual Basic application on it and a blank, formatted disk for the other drive.

Launch Visual Basic and run the program to be sure it works. Select an icon for it. (A property of the form). Remove any files your application doesn't use. Save the program as TEXT. Create an EXE file, then exit Visual Basic.

From Visual Basic program group double-click the Application Setup Wizard:
Setup Wizard has 6 steps: After completing each step click **Next**.

① **Select a project:**
Click **Select MAK File** to browse through the *.MAK files.

> **Where is the Visual Basic project file for the application that you want to distribute?**
> Project File
> _____
> ☐ **Rebuild the project's EXE file**
> [**Select MAK File**]

② **Indicate any special features your application supports:**

③ **Requires no action on your part:** Setup Wizard goes to Visual Basic to compile.

> **What features does your application support?**
> ☐ **Data Access**
> ☐ **OLE Automation**
> ☐ **Dynamic Data Exchange (DDE)**
> ☐ **Crystal Reports for Visual Basic**
> ☐ **Financial Functions**

④ **Select the drive and type for the master distribution disk:**

> **Select the floppy disk drive and the diskette type:**
> **Disk Drive:** [b: ▼]
> **Type:** [1.2 M Disk ▼]
> [**Save Template**]
> [**Open Template**]

⑤ You are asked to add or remove any additional files, then Setup goes to DOS to compress the files.

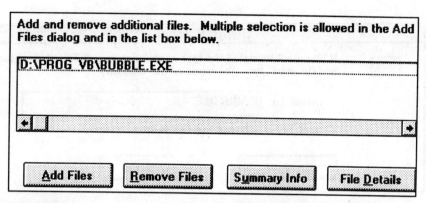

⑥ Setup tells you the number of diskettes required. Insert disk and click **OK.**

Eventually, Setup will tell you that the distribution disk master is finished.
Click **Exit.**

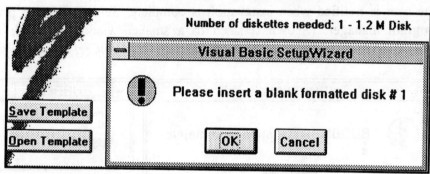

From File Manager 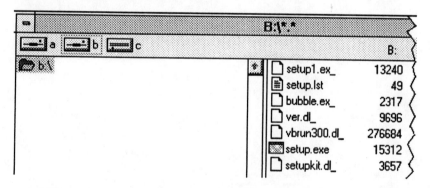, examine the files on the distribution disk: The name of the application in the example is BUBBLE. A file extension with an underscore, **bubble.ex_** for example, indicates that the file is compressed.

setup1.ex_	13240
setup.lst	49
bubble.ex_	2317
ver.dl_	9696
vbrun300.dl_	276684
setup.exe	15312
setupkit.dl_	3657

The user runs the file called SETUP.EXE to install your application. Run setup on your machine. The user is given an opportunity to select a drive:

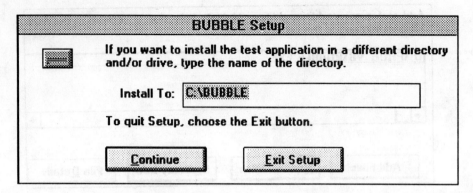

The user is notified when installation is complete, Setup creates a program group in Windows program manager. (Shown re-sized to a smaller window.) Click on the icon to run your application program! *If you forgot to select an icon, you get the default icon shown below!*

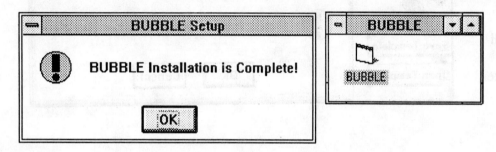

Appendix L: Programs

Index